Abundance Beyond Trauma

ABUNDANCE
Beyond Trauma

Discovering Your Courage for Change and Commitment to Yourself.

Jeannine L. Rashidi, AP

ISBN: 978-1-7366648-0-3

Free Gift

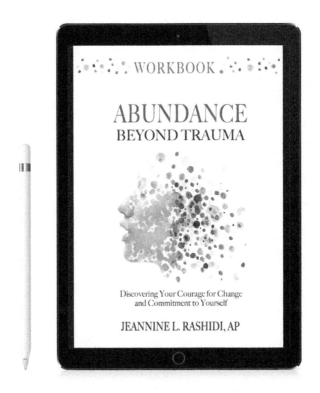

Download your free Abundance Beyond Trauma Workbook here.

https://www.goodbyetension.com/abundance-beyond-trauma

Dedication

This book is dedicated to...

My grandchildren, Xavier, Xiomara, Everley, and Layla, what an honor it is to be your grandmother. My hope for you is to learn from your ancestors' cycles and continually work toward changing the negative ones that create adverse life experiences for yourself and others. Remember the connection and power of your heart; it is your superpower.

Healing is about becoming whole again.
It's about integrating all the fragments of ourselves.
Mind, body and spirit.
It's about returning to the way we were
before we lost touch with our heart.

- Edan Harari

Acknowledgements

To my daughter's Laurel and Jillian, you are what pushed me forward every step of the way; through observing my struggles, poor choices, growth, positive choices, and accomplishments, you both learned and were inspired to keep on the healing path. Watching you both as mothers is such a joy and inspiration. Thank you for your patience, understanding, and courage through those challenging times when you were younger. May we always remember our commitment to change the cycles of dysfunction for the sake of future generations. I love you both more than words can express, and I appreciate the unique and precious gifts you have brought into this life.

To my husband, Ramiel, your love, support, and guidance have been a monumental aspect of my healing journey that I'm eternally grateful for. I am truly blessed to be part of your healing journey and continue our commitment to healing our trauma and wounds. What has blossomed between us is extraordinarily vast.

To Vaidya Jayarajan Kodikannath, your guidance and wisdom as my Ayurvedic Doctor and Teacher have been pivotal for my foundation and growth. This book couldn't have blossomed into creation without your contribution to my healing journey.

To my clients, thank you for your faith and trust. Each of you has blessed my life and journey and contributed to the fruition of this book.

TABLE OF CONTENTS

FOREWORD

Written by Vaidya Jayarajan Kodikannath BSc, BAMS, AD

Ancient healing traditions like Ayurveda empha-size that the healer is within and healing is ultimately a self-transformation process. Every individual is a unique expression of the cosmic consciousness, and the sus-tenance of life is through the seamless flow of nature through the body-mind systems in the form of food, water, breath, and perceptions. The ability to transform, purify, nurture, nourish and flow are the key indicators for healing and well-being. Since the mind and body work together as a single entity, the mind's well-being contributes to the body's strength and balance, and any disturbance in the mind can affect the body and express physical symptoms and vice versa.

Ancient texts of Ayurveda explain that 'mind care is life care' as our life is the sum of our experiences and our responses to those experiences. Every occasion creates an impression in our deeper mind, and that impression will become the yardstick for our response to similar experiences in the future. Meaning our entire behavior patterns depend on the collection of our experiences and how our mind created the series of impressions, which lead to a series of actions. Making the traumas the most difficult to cope with as the aberrations produced by such traumatic experiences become the reality of that individual's life, carried forward in every future perception and action. This pattern will be much stronger if the traumas happen during the childhood period. The most challenging part is that those who have gone through traumas may not recognize or appreciate the supportive and positive environment that may come later in their life. The hidden memories of the trauma can get triggered by words, images, touch, smell, or a taste and can make them experience the same trauma even while they are in a safe and positive environment. Such triggers are recurrent and cyclical; for example, a traumatic experience after a cake cutting on the 10th birthday can become a trigger whenever they are at a cake cutting in the future. The fascinating part of such PTSD cases is that most of them may not even recognize that it is coming from the previous trauma, and it doesn't have anything to do with their current life situation!

Based on the Ayurvedic teachings, intellectual awareness (Dhi), courage or determination (Dhriti), and spiritual awareness (Atmadi Vijnanam) are considered the most potent medicines to heal the mind from any imbalances, including those caused by trauma. Healing is the process of self-transformation through proper identification of the issue and then taking the mind-body system through purification, stabilization, and restoration.

"Abundance Beyond Trauma" is an extraordinary book that can inspire millions of people who are still in the grip of past traumas. I do not have enough words to appreciate the courage, openness, and dedication of Jeannine L. Rashidi for opening her own incredible life story of recurrent, extreme traumas for decades of her life and how she came out of her PTSD through perseverance, determination, and bold actions. As her Vaidya (Ayurvedic Doctor) and teacher, I am so proud of Jeannine. This book is a clear depiction of her passion, strength, and how one can ultimately come out of PTSD naturally and become a true healer and leader. I have not seen any such books in the area of trauma recovery with such a real story with step-by-step practical tools.

"Abundance Beyond Trauma" is the best guide available for those who have gone through traumas as well as for students, teachers, and practitioners of any healing profession. I highly recommend the book to all those who love to learn about the human mind and behaviors.

Vaidya Jayarajan Kodikannath BSc, BAMS, AD, is an Ayurvedic scholar, clinician, and educator with over 20 years of clinical experience in India and the U.S. He represents a lineage of Vaidyas in Kerala, India. He has served Kerala Ayurveda USA as Director for all academic programs and wellness services and Lead Faculty and Chief Ayurvedic Consultant since 2010. He serves on the Board of Directors for the National Ayurvedic Medical Association (NAMA), as well as the California Association of Ayurvedic Medicine (CAAM) and Board of Advisor of Association of Ayurvedic Professionals of North America (AAPNA).

INTRODUCTION:

What does it mean to be activated, charged or triggered? When we perceive an unmet need or threat, this can create an emotional response known as a trigger response. When we have adverse life experiences or trauma, it's customary to be challenged or triggered by people, places, things, words, behaviors, smells, etc. I found that I was triggered by the trauma and adverse experiences I had most of the time. I was sick and tired of being triggered, and I searched for solutions to change this trigger experience that I was having. Have you ever been emotionally challenged or triggered by something or someone, and it takes hold of you in a way that seems unmanageable, leaving you in a fight, flight, or freeze response?

I'll show you how to process through a challenging experience or trigger to feel empowered instead of debilitated, creating a deeper relationship with yourself where there's honesty and trust within.

Having lived the first 25 years of my life with severe emotional, mental, sexual, and physical abuse, I began a journey of healing and changing the dysfunctional cycles. This was happening while I was building my Health and Wellness practice, called Goodbye Tension, treating clients who also had trauma or adverse life experiences, questioning whether I was the appropriate practitioner for them, since I was still deep into my healing journey. It became clear that my experience along with my honesty, vulnerability, and authenticity with my clients were the perfect ingredients for trust and guidance in their healing journey. Thereby, I followed this path, trusting that I could help whomever came or could find a practitioner to help them. Now, 18 years later, I bring my personal and professional experience to you.

Suppose you desire to free your mind and heart from low self-esteem, scarcity, or a triggered state. In that case, this book will not only inspire you but offer you practical tools to use daily to begin changing this cycle, allowing for a healthier relationship with yourself, which leads to more beneficial relationships in general.

When I look back on where I came from, what I went through, and where I'm today, I feel compelled to share this wisdom. In the 18 years I've been in professional practice, I've had the honor of witnessing clients grow and blossom in ways they never imagined. I'll share a few of their stories in the chapters to come.

Now is the time to begin this journey. When you're healthy and balanced, your relationships become healthy and balanced, leading to healthier communities and a healthier world. The work you do with yourself will significantly impact future generations, communities, and the planet. Let's all do our part by creating the healthiest relationships possible, beginning with ourselves.

I intend to share my story on a high level. As a part of my journey, I learned that my story could create trauma for others, and I wouldn't want to do that. I want to be an inspiration for others. Thus, I won't be going into great depth or detail about each type of abuse that I experienced. Instead, I'll give you an enlightened perspective of those experiences and how I learned the cycle of dysfunction and abuse. I was motivated to break that cycle and begin my journey of healing from PTSD by stepping into my professional role as an Alternative Health and Wellness Practitioner. I guided others toward wholeness by teaching them how to have a better relationship with themselves, while on the path to becoming a Doctor of Ayurveda and aspiring motivational speaker.

You'll notice my continual reference to the Heart and Mind disconnect and restoring the Heart and Mind connection to an integrated whole.

During adverse experiences that are more than our mind-body system can handle, a disconnect can happen from the heart, mind, and/or body. The moment the disconnect happens, that aspect of you gets stuck in a past space and time. Most of the time, we're unaware that this has happened. It's not until we start noticing an imbalance within ourselves or relationships that we realize something's not quite right. For example, you may see a need for acknowledgment in your relationships, which may stem from suffering a lack of acknowledgment as a child. It could be as simple as a drawing you made for your mother, and when you went to show her, she unconsciously rejected you, as she was busy cooking dinner. She didn't intend to reject you; however, you were so open-hearted in making this drawing and offering it to her that the rejection created an adverse experience, affecting your future relationships. That aspect of you is disconnected and stuck at that moment, waiting to be acknowledged. I'll show you how to do that in the chapters to come.

My vision is to bring about a revolution in how we relate harmoniously between our Heart and Mind, with ourselves and others. It can only happen when we're willing to look at what has triggered us so that healing and integration can begin.

Yesterday I was clever so I wanted to change the world. Today I am wise, so I am changing myself.

-Rumi

How to use this book:

Each chapter is designed to help you understand adverse life experiences and the long-term effects they have on the relationship with yourself and others by using my story along with some client cases. By understanding this cycle, you can create a healthier cycle.

The images provided are to help activate different parts of the brain, especially when triggered, to try to understand what's happening. I'm a very visual and kinesthetic learner and benefit from imagery.

I provide key points at the end of each chapter. If you're in such a triggered state that reading is challenging, then review the light bulb imaged key points until you get to Chapter 7 where you can begin the Triggered Worksheet and Feelings List, which will take you to the Pocket Guide at the end of the book.

Each chapter is rich with information and its title may also guide you, depending on your current mental and emotional state.

Chapter 1

Trauma, PTSD, and Adverse Life Experiences.

Trauma[1] is an emotional response to a terrible event like an accident, rape, or natural disaster. Immediately after the event, shock and denial are typical. Longer-term reactions include unpredictable emotions, flashbacks, strained relationships, and even physical symptoms like headaches or nausea.

Post Traumatic Stress Disorder[2] is a psychiatric disorder that may occur in people who have experienced or witnessed a traumatic event such as a natural disaster, a severe accident, a terrorist act, war/combat, or rape or who have been threatened with death, sexual violence, or serious injury.

---

1   https://www.apa.org/topics/trauma
2   https://www.psychiatry.org/patients-families/ptsd

This condition may last months or years with triggers that can bring back memories of the trauma, accompanied by intense emotional, mental, and physical reactions.

Adverse Life Experiences[3]

"In recent years, the phrase *adverse life experience* has entered the discussions about both trauma and stress. It's a term that helps us to distinguish between the ordinary stressors of daily life; from the stressors that can become traumatic for some people. In a sense, adverse life experiences fall somewhere in the middle of a severity range from the extreme, catastrophic events we usually associate with post-traumatic stress disorder (PTSD), to ordinary, everyday stress. As such, adverse life experiences may not meet the diagnostic criteria for post-traumatic stress disorder (the clinical diagnosis most commonly associated with trauma)."

My personal experience definition: Events that I witnessed or was directly involved in that were too much for my Emotional Heart and Mind/psyche to process. This led to a disconnect from my Emotional Heart and Mind, leaving parts of myself stuck in a time loop of the related event. The time loop gets activated when triggered, and the emotional, mental, and physical responses are coming from that part of me that's now reliving the adverse experience. I'm no longer in presence; I'm in the past and unable to see correctly as my lens of perception is from the stuck-triggered part of me. My actions and

---

3   https://www.gracepointwellness.org/109-post-traumatic-stress-disorder/article/55727-what-are-adverse-life-experiences

reactions may be confusing and immature to others and even to myself upon reflection.

Any adverse event can create an impression that can show up later in life, creating an imbalance in our relationships. For example, an adolescent girl works incredibly hard to get good grades, and when she shows her father the report card, his response is to tell her she can do better than that. While that may be true, the adolescent girl needs acknowledgement from her father for her hard work and doesn't get that. As a married woman, she feels her best is not good enough in her marriage, career, and as a mother. Most days, she feels like giving up, as her efforts aren't recognized and she feels like a failure. While this may not seem traumatic, it certainly had a long-lasting impression.

Often, trauma can happen from someone you know, love, or trust. This was the case as I experienced ongoing psychological, mental, emotional, sexual, and physical abuse in the first 25 years of my life.

I was born into addiction and violence. My parents hadn't healed their wounds from their adverse life experiences and traumas. In recent years, I dug deeper into the family history; some of these behaviors and tendencies carried on from generation to generation. As you dive into this book, it will become even more apparent why change must happen because the cycle of abuse tends to repeat, mostly when ignored.

So why and how does trauma happen? From my experience, wounded people wound others when they haven't tended to their own wounds. A lack of relationship with oneself leads to a disconnect between the Emotional Heart and Mind due to trauma that hasn't been healed, reconciled, or digested, which leads to violence on various levels. Unresolved pain, often from trauma and adverse life experiences, leads to a disconnect in the Emotional Heart and Mind and may harm oneself and others.

The simple act or decision to avoid the pain that needs healing may lead to a disconnect from the heart to not feel the intense emotion. One essentially is heartless around this feeling. When others show up in this space around this feeling, the wounded one's responses can be numb, cold, frozen, or a desire to get out of the situation or away from the people who are comfortable in that space. The responses could also be on the other side of the spectrum with expressions of rage, anger, hatred, and desire to fight. All of these responses are pointing out the disconnect in Heart and Mind.

Charaka, one of the ancient Ayurvedic scholars, stated that "Heart is the abode (controlling organ) of the channels of circulation of rasa (plasma), vata (the elements of air and space; the principle of movement), the sattva (Mind), the buddhi (wisdom), indriya (senses), atman (soul), and ojas (vital essence)."[4]

Sushruta, the famous Ayurvedic surgeon, also stated that "Though the entire body is pervaded by consciousness, heart is the special seat thereof; along with consciousness mind is also there."[5]

---

4   Charaka Samhita, Chikitsa Sthana XXIV/34-35 By: R.K.Sharma Bhagwan Das
5   Susruta Samhita, Sarirasthana IV/30-31 By: P.V. Sharma

Hence, a disturbance to the senses and mind are directly related to the heart.

"Ayurveda (a Sanskrit word) translates to knowledge of life. Ayus stands for the combination of the body, sense organs, mind, and soul, and Veda means knowledge or wisdom"[6]

From my Ayurvedic training and personal experience, more awareness and consciousness around any adverse life experience or trauma brings about a healing to the essence of the Heart. Before the adverse or traumatic experience, there was a beautiful flow within the nature of the heart and body-mind system. The adverse experience, which wasn't digestible to the Heart and Mind, disconnected that flow. It's what I refer to as the Heart and Mind disconnect.

My Heart and Mind Disconnect

By the time I was four years old, I knew what sex was on various levels along with physical and psychological violence. The white powder (methamphetamines) that were lined up on my parents' side table was snorted. That changed their personality and behavior in a slightly different way than beer and vodka. When this change occurred, that's when the "Bad Things" also happened.

I dared one time to tell my parents that they shouldn't snort the powder or drink those things because it turns them into the "Bad Mommy and Daddy." After that, my parents started giving me a full adult size dose of Ny-

---

6 Charaka Samhita, Sutrasthana I/42 By: R.K.Sharma Bhagwan Das

Quil, which knocked me out every night. I would only have the feeling the next morning of grogginess, and my body aching in areas I would only later realize had been violated while I was passed out.

I learned to keep quiet (this would eventually lead to communication problems in relationships in my adult years) and always put a smile on my face as instructed. I discovered that there was less to deal with as long as I didn't "rock the boat" or question the adults' actions around me.

This way of life didn't stop my internal questioning; in fact, not expressing my questions only amplified them. Why do they snort the white powder when it always ends up in craziness? Why do we go to church and learn how to live a wholesome life just to come home and live the opposite? Why do my parents use such vulgar language and then reprimand me if I use the same words? Why do they smile and act as if they like people only to speak poorly about them behind their back? Why do I feel that the only way to receive love is to do those things that feel wrong? Do all families have this dynamic? How was I going to get out of here?

My first attempt at running away, well, it was more of being thrown out actually, was at seven years old. I had been saving money in a jar for over a year and had it hidden in my closet. If my parents left money out, I would take it and put it in my jar.

My mother was coming down from Meth, and, to this day, I don't know what triggered her, but I remember what she said quite vividly.

"You seduced your father!" I had no idea what the word seduced meant, although I had a vague memory of hearing the word used in my direction at some point while dancing freely at around six years old. Looking back, this accusation seemed odd considering both of the parent's involvement in this type of abuse. In her rage, she pushed me into the bathroom, slamming my head against the porcelain toilet, yelling, "Get out of my house!". I left with my jar of money and knocked on the neighbor's door to use their phone to call my friend to pick me up. Looking back, the fact that I knew I needed to save money to leave was way beyond what any child should have to conceive. I remember expressing to my friend's mom that I would need to use the money to get the stitches removed from my ankle, where I had fallen a few weeks prior. Why the cops were never called by the neighbor or my friend's mom is still a wonder to me. I know that after my friend's mom spoke with mine on the phone, I was returned home.

I often had many "Why?" Questions and was very confused by the response to these questions. The response to these questions led me to question myself and my understanding of life. You see, we depend on our parents to teach us about life and to guide us toward being contributing members of society one day, to love, question, discern, etc. But when the parents are so far out of balance that their responses to my questions had everything to do with their self-preservation and justification of their lifestyle and nothing to do with my health and wellness, it got pretty confusing internally. What I knew for sure was wrong, I was told was, in fact, right, and this is how internal doubt grew from as far back as I can remember.

I witnessed physical and verbal fighting regularly between my parents, which often ended with my dad leaving and my mother throwing heavy objects, like a TV at him on his way out. My mother would be so angry and then tell me that only I could bring him back. She and I would get in the car and go driving around town looking for him. Once we found him, she would drop me off and park up the street. I would convince him to come back, and, of course, he always did. Again, this wasn't something a child should be involved in.

I remember when my dad said, "If your mother says that the wall is purple (it was white), then the wall is purple!" That's when I realized that I was living in insanity and needed an exit strategy.

We had all sorts of people at our house, many of whom were biker gang members who supplied my parents with drugs. The parties lasted days, with kids running around without supervision for extended periods.

Now I was fortunate that I had some excellent teachers in school, suspicious of what was going on at home and with their love, help, and support, I learned how to focus on my studies, managing a 4.0 GPA with an aspiration to go to college and be in a profession that allowed me to help people, but mainly because I also needed help. I asked myself, "What type of profession will help people who are in situations that are so unhealthy and are trying to get out? Doctor maybe?"

I got my emotional needs met by my teachers. They would set up after-school time to come in and do my homework while they graded papers. I would enjoy the conversation and a healthy time with them. My teachers taught me how to ask for financial assistance to be part of the extracurricular activities like music and sports. My mother wanted me to play the violin as she did in school, so I did, partly because I wanted her to be happy and somewhat because I didn't feel like I had a choice. My music teacher saw something in me and later asked me to learn how to play the electric bass for the jazz band and the upright bass for orchestra, which meant practicing every day before and after school. That meant less time at home. I joined the choir, the dance team, volleyball, along with track and field, which filled up a lot of time. Of course, part of me wanted my parents to be proud of me and at the same time I dreaded emotional outbursts or inappropriate comments at any school event. I was so desperately wanting a healthy mother and father like the ones I observed through my friends.

I felt very awkward as a kid, and it seemed to stand out more to me in my friendships. I was quite over-weight and couldn't relate to my peers. Their troubles, concerns, aspirations, etc., were so different from mine that it was clear I had a very different life than anyone else I knew. I was always grateful to be invited to birthday parties or sleepovers, which pointed out how incredibly different my home environment was. I remember asking at a sleepover if the parents were going to be sleeping with us, and my friends laughed and looked at me in a very peculiar way. I never had sleepovers for apparent reasons, and the kids who lived on our street always joked about how they could hear my mother yelling throughout the entire block. The one time my best friend lent me some clothes, my mother's insecurity and rage were so intense that she drove to my friend's house and threw the borrowed clothes on the lawn, yelling that her daughter didn't need anything from anyone but her.

Thank goodness for the friends who knew how crazy my parents were and still decided to be my friend.

By the time I entered high school, I was hoping that a class would teach me how to deal with what was going on at home. Unfortunately, there was no such class. And even though I was a straight-A student destined to get a college scholarship. The idea of staying long enough to complete that process felt like an eternity. I felt anything would be better than my home life. I had run away from home a few times and always ended up caught and having to return. At one point, a police officer pulled me aside and said, "We don't have enough concrete evidence to get your parents the help they need even though I can see that you also need help."

I realized that I was unwilling to wait around for the system or play this silly game of going to a therapist in front of whom my parents were so great at making themselves look like innocent angels and portraying me as the crazy one. Part of the illness of a dysfunctional home is being taught how to put on a perfect show for the world so that no one can see how crazy things are behind closed doors. It's quite brilliant; this way, when you dare to speak up, it seems way out of left field. As an adult, this learned behavior came into my relationships when I portrayed continuous happiness while losing it on the inside, which led to emotional outbursts of intense anger. I thought to myself, *How many CPS and teacher reports does it take before someone comes and helps me?*

After the first semester of 10th grade at 15 years old, I successfully ran away from home and hitchhiked 400 miles away. I learned how to live homelessly and avoid getting caught by the authorities. I was never going back. Or so I thought.

 Any adverse event can create an impression that can show up later in life, creating an imbalance that will affect our relationship with ourselves and others.

 Wounded people, wound others when they haven't tended to their own wounds.

Chapter 2

Cycles and Disease

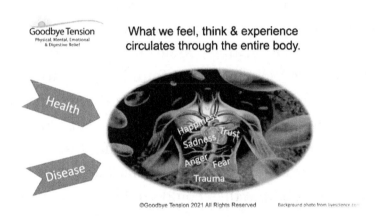

Goodbye Tension
Physical, Mental, Emotional
& Digestive Relief

What we feel, think & experience circulates through the entire body.

Health

Happiness
Sadness
Trust
Anger
Fear
Trauma

Disease

©Goodbye Tension 2021 All Rights Reserved   Background photo from livescience.com

Experiencing or witnessing something horrifying or adverse can create a feeling of insecurity, fear, and intensity that's too much to process or digest mentally and emotionally, creating a split/disconnect. What we think and feel can create ease or dis-ease within our entire being. It's circulating in our blood. In essence, there's a disconnect in the Heart and Mind channel, a divorce, if you will, within you, within the self—a continual pulling in opposite directions, leading to discord and even disease.

Living homeless, I learned many, valuable survival skills. I endured more trauma from that experience as well.

I learned where the soup kitchens were and which fast-food restaurants threw away perfectly good food into the dumpsters at night. Since I was near a beach, I bathed there as well as washed my clothes. I certainly didn't want to look homeless or create any suspicion for a police officer to pull over and question me. In the winter, the Salvation Army had a shelter for women and children. I lied about my age, and managed to get away with the story that my purse and belongings had been stolen. This story allowed me to get clothing from the shelter as well as breakfast and dinner.

I met some fascinating people during that time, many of whom were Vietnam Vets. I found it fascinating how easy it was for me to be around them in their drunken stupor. Many of these veterans chose to be homeless as part of some anti-government belief that I didn't comprehend at the time. I felt safe with them, and a few pointed out, early on, that they could see I had been through something in life that they understood all too well: trauma. Some days, I witnessed flashbacks when they would remember their time in the Vietnam war. The alcohol and drugs took away their pain long enough to get some relief from the flashbacks. Watching them often made me wonder what my parents must have been trying to relieve with their addiction. I minimized my experiences since I hadn't been in a war; I felt my trauma was somehow less than theirs. Not that you can compare experiences, but I did. We all lived as a small community in what we called "The Jungle," which was just a strip of land with many trees where our tents were hidden. There was an understanding of space and watching over the community, so outsiders didn't find our belongings.

There was always drama, though, as everyone had trust issues because of our trauma, and those moments created even more trauma.

During that time, I entered into a relationship with a man 17 years my senior; he also came from childhood abuse. I was unaware at that point that I was entering into a relationship that would be precisely what I had run away from.

I hadn't dealt with my previous experiences yet; I had only run away from the situation, and I still had all those dysfunctional impressions. My standard was dysfunctional, so statistically[1], I would either end up in a similar situation or, worse, become the abuser. Why is that? I left home intending to create a better life for myself, as best a 15-year-old girl on her own could, only to fall right back into that same pattern. Subconsciously and unconsciously, I was still in a victim mindset; a victim needs a perpetrator, and a perpetrator needs a victim. I don't want that previous statement to be triggering, so allow me to explain. If I have the victim's energy, that energy needs the perpetrator's power to maintain the state of victimhood and vice versa. If there's no perpetrator, there's no victim.

I was trying to heal my inner victim from the experiences impressed upon me by said perpetrators. If I healed that inner victim, there would no longer be space

---

1   https://americanspcc.org/child-abuse-statistics/

for a perpetrator. Since I hadn't recovered that part of me, I naturally attracted the same thing into my life that I had left at home.

Richard (I have changed his name for the purpose of this book) and I connected through our pain, and I believed him when he said he would never turn out like his dad, who was an abusive alcoholic, among other abuses. We lived together in the Jungle during the dry months, and I went to the shelter during the wet months. After some time, I noticed Richard's claimed occasional drug use was a habit, his drug of choice being the same as my parents, Methamphetamines. Each time he got high, there was more abusive behavior, and when I asked him to quit, I believed him when he said he would, which was an improvement from my attempts at being able to request that from my parents. As you can see, I'm continually trying to find the positive by comparing it to the worst I had experienced, instead of seeing all of this as dysfunction—a survival mindset and not a thriving mindset, which I'll discuss later.

Being that I hadn't healed my childhood trauma, I believed the first man or woman to tell me they loved me. Why? Starving for love and desperately needing it, these words utterly blinded me. Also, my understanding of love, thus far, was from a place of dysfunction.

I got pregnant when I was 15 and lost that pregnancy, which was more physically painful than emotionally at the time, only because I wasn't in a place to be in touch with my feelings yet. It was terrifying to live homeless, worried that I would get caught and have to go home, as well as the dysfunction I was currently living in. I got pregnant again at 16 and was deathly afraid that the police were looking for me and would ultimately send me back home. I was homeless, living on the beach, hoping something would change. Richard said he was looking for work, and yet what money he did make, he was spending on his habit. I risked getting caught as a runaway by getting a job at a movie theatre. I just knew that I needed to provide for my baby. I made $4.25/hour, which paid for the weekly hotel rent. My food consisted of whatever the Women Infants and Children program provided. Eggs, milk, cereal, cheese, and peanut butter. I also took home whatever the theatre was to throw out at the end of the day. The moment I received my paycheck, I immediately paid for the hotel rent; otherwise, Richard would have spent it on his habit.

Then came the biker gangs, who made the Meth, whom Richard helped by getting the supplies they needed, which supported his addiction. One biker, whom I will call Philip, approached me after watching a physical and verbal altercation between Richard and me. He offered to "take care of Richard," which meant to make him disappear and that he would take care of my unborn child and me. While I was incredibly tempted, Philip's life wasn't an improvement from the present situation except that he may have been kinder. He rode with the gang, made Meth, sold it, and was always on the move.

By the time I went into labor, the relationship with Richard was just like my childhood. The house that Richard and I were renting a room from was in eviction, and with nowhere to live, I had no choice but to go back home once my daughter was born. Believe it or not, I still felt safer with Richard being with me coming back home.

Returning home was the equivalent of a horror film that creates a sequel, and the sequel is never as good as the original; it's usually worse. I combined two hells into one big one. It was massive chaos. Drugs were everywhere. Now all the addicts were scoring for each other. Then the lack of trust created violence, and the cycle continued.

My childhood wounds hadn't been healed, and now I had even more.

I was 17, working full time to make money quickly to move out while my parents were trying to get Richard thrown in jail for statutory rape. That's ironic, looking back at it. Since I knew I was heading back home after I gave birth, and knowing my parents, I intentionally didn't put a name for the father on the birth certificate to protect him from what I suspected may happen. To protect Richard and get out from being the ward of my parents, I married at 17. I should also mention that I genuinely believed that the institution of marriage and saying "I do" carried some magical powers where you live happily ever after. Oh, how naive I was, believing that was true, but It would take me eight more years from this point to leave this situation.

As I write this, I have to share the laughter and tears of this tangled web with you that I struggled to get out of and ended up even more entangled time and time again.

Richard made promises of getting clean and sober throughout the years and had periods of a few months when he managed to stay clean. Usually, once he got triggered, he would relapse. I would sometimes respond with compassion, but, other times, I had incredible anger. Naturally, I was triggered by this and was getting quite tired of drugs, violence, dysfunction, etc., and feeling like my life would never elevate with what felt like an anchor around my neck.

I had made a few attempts to leave the relationship and was unsuccessful. I had gotten as far as finding a place to live and then found out I was pregnant again at 19. The fear of being pregnant with a 3-year-old trying to provide and live on my own (I didn't realize at that point I was already doing this.) prevented me from leaving. I considered aborting since I couldn't imagine bringing another child into this situation. I had made the appointment, but when I arrived at the waiting room, I just couldn't do it. The expression "Damned if I do and damned if I don't" fits perfectly here.

Since I was the sole provider, I wasn't home much. I managed to climb somewhat of the corporate ladder from Telemarketer to VP of Marketing. My career was where I discovered that I had a real skill for motivating, inspiring, communicating, and training others. I hired people who were trying to make a change in their life and I enjoyed watching them succeed. This trait is essential, as it's still a critical motivating factor for me. Anyone willing to make changes for their betterment inspires me, and if I can help, I will.

I saw the potential in Richard, which was quite different from reality. It was one thing for me to see his potential and another for him to realize it. Only he could help himself. It had to come from within; otherwise, I was trying to drag him uphill when he had no interest in climbing that hill.

Having the discernment to know when to step away is critical. The challenge can be the illusion of how you want something to be vs. how it is.

Meanwhile, history was repeating itself at home. My daughters were seeing their mom abused in various ways, and, eventually, they started to show signs that were all too familiar to me, physically, psychologically, emotionally, and sexually. My heart broke. I was supposed to leave home and meet my knight in shining armor who would rescue me, and we would start a family and live happily ever after. I would eventually realize that I had to be my own rescuer and my knight in shining armor if this would ever change.

One day I came across the most fantastic book, *7 Habits of Highly Effective People* by Stephen Covey. This book motivated and inspired me in ways I could have never imagined during a very dark time.

Having quit my job to stay home to keep my daughters safe and figure out how to leave, I remember the moment when I found "the center in the storm."[2] Richard left the house that day claiming to look for work, which usually meant scoring drugs and having sex with anyone willing, only to return home, claiming no work was found. While he was out, I grabbed my new book and took both the girls to the pool. It was just the three of us. While the girls played, I sat and read. The silence that surrounded me was profound as if I had entered a room with no distractions of drama or trauma, yet I knew the storm was still around me. After the first day, I realized that I needed to read and contemplate alone by the pool while the girls played daily. What was happening was incredible. The more time I spent not managing Richard, filling my brain with wisdom from Stephen Covey's book, and spending time in contemplation, the clearer it became on how to move out of the storm. By staying so centered and concentrated each day, I was able to see the storm around me instead of being pulled in by the storm.

Below in italics are quotes from the part of the book that most struck me. My responses are in regular text:

Independence[3]

*The first three habits surround moving from dependence to independence (i.e., **self-mastery**):*

---

2   https://en.wikipedia.org/wiki/Eye_of_the_Storm
3   https://en.wikipedia.org/wiki/The_7_Habits_of_Highly_Effective_People

I had never heard this word "Self-Mastery" and when I read it for the first time, I got goosebumps and a rush of energy with the awareness that this was what I wanted.

1 - Be proactive

Take responsibility for your reaction to your experiences, take the initiative to respond positively and improve the situation. Recognize your Circle of Influence and Circle of Concern. Focus your responses and initiates on the center of your influence and constantly work to expand it. Don't sit and wait in a reactive mode, waiting for problems to happen (Circle of Concern) before taking action.

I'm 25 with the realization that my whole life was a reaction after reaction with a lovely intention that needed so much more support behind it.

2 - Begin with the end in mind

Envision what you want in the future so you can work and plan towards it. Understand how people make decisions in their life. To be effective you need to act based on principles and constantly review your mission statements. Are you - right now - who you want to be? What do I have to say about myself? How do you want to be remembered? If habit 1 advises changing your life to act and be proactive, habit 2 advises that you are the programmer! Grow and stay humble.

I wanted a healthy and balanced life. The person I'm married to is not in a place to be a part of that vision. I decided to be in this relationship based on my needs and codependencies. I need to work on my needs and codependency to be in a healthier relationship. My mission is to change this cycle of dysfunction that has repeated itself so that it doesn't continue in my daughters; lives.

I'm not who I want to be yet, and I believe I can be. I want to be remembered as someone who overcame adversity by taking responsibility for my life. I haven't healed from my childhood wounds, which must be a priority for change to happen. I'm the programmer of my life. It's time to reset the operating system.

All things are created twice. Before we act, we should act in our minds first. Before we create something, we measure twice. This is what the principle is about. Do not just act; think first: Is this how I want it to go, and are these the correct consequences.

3 - First things first

Talk about what is important and what is urgent. Priority should be given in the following order

-Important deadline & crises

-Long-term development

-Distractions & deadlines

-Frivolous distractions

-The Important deadline and crisis at that moment was to protect myself and my daughters from further abuse and figure out how to get out.

-Long-term development was to get help with healing these adverse experiences and trauma. The distractions are the relationships that enforce the cycle of dysfunction and the deadline to end these types of distractions ASAP.

-Frivolous distractions included any drama that would distract me from my mission.

Next came Interdependence, which kept swirling around in my thoughts. What does that even look like from the perspective of a 25-year-old PTSD mind and now mother of two? I didn't know what this would look like, yet I knew my life needed this.

Interdependence

The next three habits talk about Interdependence (e.g., working with others):

4 - Think win-win

Genuine feelings for mutually beneficial solutions or agreements in your relationships. Value and respect people by understanding a "win" for all is ultimately a better long-term resolution than if only one person in the situation had gotten their way. Think Win-Win isn't about being nice, nor is it a quick-fix technique. It is a character-based code for human interaction and collaboration.

5 - Seek first to understand, then to be understood.

Use empathetic listening to genuinely understand a person, which compels them to reciprocate the listening and take an open mind to be influenced by you. This creates an atmosphere of caring, and positive problem-solving.

Habit 5 is greatly embraced in the Greek philosophy represented by 3 words:

1) Ethos -- your personal credibility. It's the trust that you inspire, your Emotional Bank Account.

2) Pathos is the empathetic side -- it's the alignment with the emotional trust of another person's communication.

3) Logos is the logic -- the reasoning part of the presentation.

The order is important: ethos, pathos, logos -- your character, and your relationships, and then the logic of your presentation.

6 - Synergize!

Combine the strengths of people through positive teamwork to achieve goals that no one could have done alone.

Continual improvement

The final habit is that of continuous improvement in both the personal and interpersonal spheres of influence.

7 - Sharpen the Saw; Growth

See also: Kaizen (continuous improvement)

Balance and renew your resources, energy, and health to create a sustainable, long-term, effective lifestyle. It primarily emphasizes exercise for physical renewal, good prayer (meditation, yoga, etc.) and good reading for mental renewal. It also mentions service to society for spiritual renewal.

Interdependence sounded like a fairytale to me. I could only fantasize about what this type of relationship might be. It did give me hope and inspiration for the future.

I had tried to leave my husband multiple times and was unsuccessful. Each time I tried to leave was more challenging than the prior because he was aware that I was trying to escape. I immediately left my job so that he was never alone with the kids. While I collected unemployment, my daughters and I would role-play all the scenarios on how to escape from the 2nd-floor apartment and get into the car; meanwhile, I was very strategically moving the bare necessities and storing them at my grandparent's house a mile away. The eldest knew what we were preparing for, and the youngest thought we were playing. Teaching my children how to escape from a dangerous situation wasn't how I had envisioned their life or mine.

I had taken very long mental notes (I was deathly afraid my husband would find the notes if I wrote them) of steps 1-3 of Stephen Covey's book.

Each day, my husband would leave to score his dope, and I would read, plan, and role-play the escape day.

The day finally came; I was waiting for the mail to arrive with my unemployment check, which was the only money I had. Well, on that particular week, the check didn't come on time. Now I was stuck in a very compromising situation. I had to wait another day for the unemployment check, or so I thought. The two backpacks by the front door had birth certificates and social security cards, etc., the final items we needed to take with us. Enough was missing from the girls' closet that it was becoming evident that leaving was going to happen, and I dreaded my husband figuring it out.

I had put both girls asleep in the front room near the front door with their shoes on so we could get out quickly, and, of course, Richard took them off once he noticed it. I thought, worse case, we leave with no shoes.

Richard's drug of choice was Meth, and throughout our relationship, he would sneak it into my drinks, and I would end up wired and up all night like he was. I had taught myself how to counteract this drug's effects on my mind and body by learning to use the opposite qualities. When I felt wired, I would continually imagine myself calm. I would slow down my breath even though my heart was beating rapidly, and, eventually, my heart would calm down. I could even make myself sleep. I realize now that I was learning to meditate, and with the wisdom of learning to act first in my mind, I was conquering the annoyance of being high against my will.

That evening, I realized I would need to use all my skills to distract Richard from noticing how much was missing from the house to make sure my plan would work. I joined him in getting high that night and made sure he was distracted. He watched me snort a line, which built his trust so that the girls sleeping in the front room were safe from him removing their shoes again and him noticing how much was missing from their room. By the time the sun came up, in one of his usual paranoid moments, he frantically told me to move the minivan, which was a month late on payment, since he had stolen the money I was hiding under the carpet for the payment. He thought he heard a tow truck and that the car was going to be under repossession. We lived in a cul de sac, and there was only one way in and out of the apartment complex. The van parked on the street was the ideal place, but I didn't want him to be suspicious, so I went to move it. The girls were still asleep with their shoes on, and it was too early for the mail to have come.

As I pulled into the driveway, both girls were standing in the driveway, crying that they had awakened with their dad yelling and hitting them and sending them out of the apartment. This was the moment; Inside, I heard God or my Higher Self say, "This is it! You have to go now."

I used the code word "BLUEBERRIES," and the girls jumped into the van. I looked at my eldest, who was extremely frightened, and explained that I had to get the two backpacks that were upstairs and that no matter what she saw or heard, she was only to unlock the car door if it was me or the police.

I ran up the stairs, and Richard was standing in the doorway, asking me what I was doing. I had been training myself for this moment. I had to convey ease and calm when I felt scared, nervous, and pumped up on adrenaline. I calmly flirted with him, explaining I was taking the girls to the babysitter so he and I could "party" all day and get high. He said, "Okay, I'll go with you!" Since he had no shoes on, which were in the farthest room in the apartment, I said, "That sounds great; get your shoes."

As he ran to get his shoes, I grabbed the two backpacks and ran so fast down the stairs that my feet went out from under me as I fell to the bottom. My daughter saw me with big, worried eyes, and I motioned for her to unlock the parked car that was on and running. I jumped in, put the car in reverse, and headed to grab our things from my grandparent's home one mile away. I called grandpa from my cell phone, frantic that my husband would check their home first, as he could easily run a 7.5-minute mile, so I only had about 7 minutes to grab and go, and I still had no money. I backed into their driveway, where they were standing ready for me. We loaded up the car, and Grandpa handed me a fistful of cash and said, "Go! We'll call the police if he shows up here!"

As I drove, I started feeling bad for my husband; who would take care of him? Yes, I genuinely thought this. Years of abuse and finally in the getaway phase, and I was thinking of him. This is the dysfunction of abuse; I felt the same way when I ran away from home. The real kicker to this story is where I would try to start a new life for myself and my kids.

I was going back to live with my parents.

The perfect example of how to use the phrase "The lesser of two evils." Since, at that point, it seemed my parents were in recovery from their addictions and supposedly working with therapists, etc., I had hope for normalcy with them, which was better than the current situation with my husband, anyway.

I was still entangled.

What I had wanted my whole life was a mom and dad who loved me. They cared for me the only way they knew, and, unfortunately, it wasn't healthy or appropriate.

I planned to save money and move out ASAP.

I did precisely that.

By this time, I was on the verge of morbid obesity at 240 pounds with hypertension, insomnia, irregular periods, severe flashbacks on top of the ones that were there from childhood. Intense fear, unwanted thoughts, hypervigilance, and night terrors had been a constant since my earliest recollection of 2 years old. I had Anxiety and Depression. I was losing chunks of time due to the PTSD episodes, and I was a smoker. I was suspicious of everyone and rightfully so. My first initiation with the feminine was through the mother relationship and the masculine initiation through the father relationship. There was never trust or security established there from the moment of my birth, I imagine. My first deeply intimate relationship was also a horrific experience. I again didn't trust myself after all this, as my decisions led me to this point. I had no confidence in my ability to get out of these cycles, yet there was always an inner voice driving me forward to keep trying for my sake and my daughters' sake.

My entire being showed all the signs of undigestible experiences. When what has been seen, felt, thought, and experienced is too intense for the psyche to comprehend, it leaves undigestible impressions in the body and mind, creating disease—yet another statistic of trauma. Twenty-five years of severe trauma was circulating throughout my bloodstream, and who governs circulation? The heart. My Heart and Mind had split; they were not relating well at all. I needed to figure out how to connect differently, and my whole life thus far had shown me what not to do. So, I just had to figure out what to do.

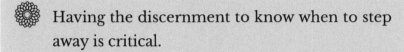 Having the discernment to know when to step away is critical.

The challenge can be the illusion of how you want something to be vs. how it is.

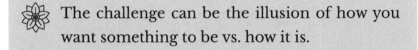 When what has been seen, felt, thought, and experienced is too intense for the psyche to comprehend, it leaves undigestible impressions in the body and mind, creating disease—yet another statistic of trauma.

Self-mastery begins with being proactive, beginning with the end in mind and knowing which priorities come first.

Chapter 3

Relating and Relationships

A relationship is a state of being connected.

I immediately found therapists for all of us, intending to change the dysfunction cycle and get to the root of this problem. As I would start opening up to my therapist, the look of horror on their face told me it was too much to hear. I was referred to many more psychologists and nearly the same thing would happen until I ended up with a psychiatrist who prescribed Zoloft and Prozac at different times. She couldn't give me a clear answer on how to heal and get to the core of this cycle of dysfunction beyond being dependent on psychiatric drugs. These drugs only numbed me; I didn't feel good or bad.

Interestingly, most of the females in my family have been on these two drugs for decades with no change in their life circumstances or behavior accountability. I expected more from these professionals, but it was clear that I wouldn't find it.

I did finally find some alternative help from therapists who worked in conjunction with alternative healers. I discovered that it would take a community to help me, as it was just too much for only one person.

As I began the healing, I decided I needed a profession in which I could create my hours to take my daughters to school, extracurricular activities, etc. I quickly found a sales job to start generating income and signed up for massage school. Never having received a massage, this was just a logical decision. I knew how to sell and market, so I felt I could figure this out as my own business.

I went to massage school from 6 am to 10 am, worked my sales job from 10 am to 5 pm came home, spent time with my daughters, and then started seeing clients for massage from 6:30 to 10 pm

During my massage training, I noticed my body was stiff, rigid, and very guarded. I would either pass out immediately or start remembering trauma and start crying while trying to enjoy a massage. Yet, at the end of most sessions, I felt improved somehow.

I was observing and feeling the conditioning of 25 years of trauma and dysfunction. While I received a massage, I started becoming aware of my thoughts and feelings and my inner dialogue. Boy, did I have a lot of self-judgment about my body, mind, and emotions. I was downright mean to myself, which again was learned behavior. Since I had the best examples of what not to do in life and relationships, I just had to figure out the opposite. That's a unique gift. That's the gift I received from my past.

I realized that I needed to create a healthier relationship with myself if any of these cycles were going to change.

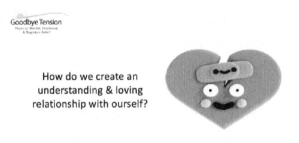

I needed courage and commitment, which created this nervous, excited, scary feeling in my heart and gut. The interesting thing about fear and excitement, for me anyway, is that it's a fine line. The feeling has similar sensations, and only when I was on the other side of that line did I realize that I ended up in fear or excitement. This feeling was a very triggering feeling. It reminded me of my trauma. So here I was, trying to change and grow, and my experience was triggering me. That strong inner voice that led me to leave at 15 and again at 25 came through, and I stayed with courage and commitment to push through the triggering feeling.

I explored my emotions, feelings, habits, thoughts, tendencies, the types of people I was attracted to, etc. I noticed that I had developed some fantastic skills during those first 25 years of life. The wall I built around my heart was thick, steel, and impenetrable. No one could get in; that way, I could never be vulnerable and hurt again. I would later discover that I was holding my own emotions hostage within this wall. The intricate maze I created in my mind was set up for every possible scenario so that no one would ever know all of me. I had learned that the more people know, the more they can manipulate and destroy. I was determined never to let that happen again. I would discover that this belief prevented me from having deep, meaningful relationships, including the most important one, with ME.

Imagine trying to be in a relationship where your partner is always searching for the harm they believe you'll eventually do to them—the entire relationship circles around this belief. When the lightbulb finally turned on, imagine my surprise when I was able to see myself and others through a new lens.

I love photography, as each lens shows you a different perspective. Some offer a broad picture, while others can hone in at a micro view. I didn't realize this at the time, but I needed not only new metaphorical lenses but also an upgraded metaphorical camera. In the future, I would come to know that lenses continually need cleaning and cameras updated as things are always changing, and upgrading is inevitable to grow.

My exploration of "relationships" led to so many beautiful discoveries.

The fantastic skills that kept me alive for 25 years were now harmful. I needed to learn something different; an upgrade was required. That camera was outdated, and the lenses were too scratched to see through. This change frightened me. Being a survivor with extraordinary abilities to foresee all the possible scenarios of harm, the ability to just up and leave, and projection of the past onto others had become a norm.

My identity was wrapped up in these skills; I would never be hurt again, or so I thought. I was truly humbled when I realized that I was now creating harm with these skills. These skills only work when you're in dangerous and dysfunctional situations. They don't work in healthy, functional relationships.

I was going to have to put those skills to rest.

Who would I be without them?

More importantly, who would I be without my story?

What if who I become, as a result, doesn't support my current life?

This line of questioning freaked me out until I was able to ask myself who I would be if I weren't triggered all the time? Then I remembered my mental notes from Stephen Covey's book, that all my life decisions came from being triggered. I only knew the triggered version of me. I knew that I didn't want to be triggered, which kept me moving forward toward change.

I had to change how I was relating to my story. For there to be a victim, there needs to be a perpetrator and vice versa. That's how I ended up in my first marriage; I was still in the victim mindset attracting the other side of the same coin, the perpetrator. I had to learn how to step out of the victim role as well as not become the perpetrator.[1] In no way does this excuse others' behavior and actions; however, it does allow for the possibility of changing a cycle, which was my first commitment in this new life I was trying to create. Taking full responsibility for the roles I step into subconsciously and unconsciously by creating a more conscious life.

I began recognizing what I learned during those 25 years. I noticed the words I used pointed out where I was still in a victim mindset. The more I discovered during this exploration, the more I realized the disconnect from my true essence. I was on a journey to connect with that essence—the nature of the heart.

What tends to happen during traumatic events is a disconnection from the parts that are too much to bear, they become undigestible experiences, and those parts of me were disconnected and stuck in their time loops. Depending on the trigger that particular version would activate, the traumatic time loop would replay and unconsciously come through my thoughts, actions, behaviors, and beliefs.

I needed to heal all those separate parts of me so that I could become more whole.

How was this going to happen?

Healing is about becoming whole again. It's about integrating all the fragments of ourselves. Mind, body, and spirit. It's about returning to the way we were before we lost touch with our heart.

—Edan Harari

---

1   https://www.kevinathompson.com/when-victims-become-perpetrators

I realized that I needed to create a healthier relationship with myself if any of these cycles were going to change.

 Taking full responsibility for the roles I step into subconsciously and unconsciously by creating a more conscious life.

Chapter 4

Courage, Commitment, and Change

Courage:[1] mental or moral strength to venture, persevere, and withstand danger, fear, or difficulty.

My drive for courage was first motivated by committing myself to not repeating these dysfunctional cycles. I wanted my daughters to finish high school, not become teen moms, and find partners who were healthier than what I had found the first time. I also wanted a more beneficial partner, but I first had to become healthier if there would be any hope of change. My commitment was that No Matter What, be willing to see the dysfunction and call it out so that I could witness it. Once observed, then change could happen. I had to question everything. My beliefs, thoughts, actions, dreams, etc. had to be reexam-

---

1   https://www.merriam-webster.com/dictionary/courage

ined. The first step was to see myself where I was. Since my formative years and early adulthood were all dysfunctional, I realized that this was all I knew with a few glimpses that not everyone has had this in their lives.

You can only begin a journey from where you are.

I had become a master of illusion. At a very young age, I learned how to act like everything was okay, even though it wasn't. I used those same skills in my first marriage as well. It had become embarrassing, as if I believed all this were somehow a reflection of me. Eventually, I would see my role in my life based on where I was, what wasn't resolved, and how that determined my decisions in all aspects of life. I would then need to learn to forgive myself.

This illusion had become so much a part of me that I believed it. I thought I was okay now that I had left the marriage and ended up back home. I was avoiding the parts of me that were so disappointed in my life. I was back home with my parents and worried about what dysfunction would carry over to my daughters, yet I had nowhere else to go at that point, so this decision came from a place of survival.

Living from a mindset of surviving is far from thriving.

I was far from okay, and the illusion of the belief that I was okay came with consequences. I still very much wanted/needed healthy parents, but there was work required, and not everyone is up to the challenge of working on themselves. It takes a certain amount of bravery, as you may not like what you see. It would take yet another seven years to realize that the path of healing wouldn't be shared with them.

I was a mess on the inside with the appearance of strength and stability on the outside. I wanted my daughters to feel stable and not worry about their mom. They had seen enough of their mother's abuse as well as their own experiences of abuse. I didn't want to break down and cry in front of them; I believed that crying was a weakness. I assure you that I was so very wrong about that belief. Because of that belief, I feel I failed my daughters in Heart during that time. I couldn't acknowledge my own Heart and, therefore, couldn't hold space for theirs. I also had the belief that emotions create confusion and lead to poor choices. From my experience, this seemed accurate. This belief meant avoiding my Heart. I was essentially Heartless, not by intention but by my unquestioned belief.

One of the first commitments I made toward health was to start losing weight. I had ended up 240 pounds with hypertension, and I realized that I wanted to be an active mother who could participate with my children. I used various diet methods to lose some of the weight, mainly the high protein, low carb style. What was interesting to me were the memories that started coming up. As the pounds came off, I began to become aware of why the weight had come on in the first place. I was holding on to trauma, physically, holding on to all of it. Obesity, hypertension, diabetes, anxiety, and depression were yet another cycle in the family line. I was headed in that direction if I wasn't willing to change. As the weight slowly came off, I became more active, and this victory gave me hope. This phase of my life also pointed out my addictive tendencies as I became obsessed with weight loss. The pendulum swung to the other side. Of course, I needed to lose some weight. But I took it too far and a bit too extreme with my 2 hours per day of intense work-outs, high protein, low carb, no fruit, and a gallon or two of water. I completely depleted my system with my radical approach. Sure, I had reached that magical number on the scale that the medical charts said I should be at, but it came with a cost.

Throughout my life, I have come to accept that this is my tendency. My love for Ayurveda's science and art spoke profoundly to me as it is about a middle way. The beauty of understanding my tendencies was that both ends of the spectrum created the space, and I needed to figure out how to stand in the middle of those two ends. I eventually lost 90 pounds and got to my goal weight, which the medical charts said I should be, yet I had no energy. I would later learn from Ayurveda that my Ojas was low. My anxiety was worse than it had ever been with migraines three to four times a month, lasting three to four days at a time, and I had severe adrenal fatigue. It would take a few years to realize that a change needed to happen around my relationship with my body and weight to get to a place of balance, a middle path. On the flip side, my heart rate was now that of an athlete's, yet my obsession with my body and weight was quite heartless. I was abusing myself physically, mentally, emotionally, and digestively to get to this goal weight. Again, the pattern was repeating itself.

The discovery of alternative healing types led to practitioners who had the skills for the various aspects of my being. Mental, emotional, physical, and spiritual. I had two alternative psychologists, who used a therapy style that was to say back to me everything I had said in a session. Hearing my story from someone else was quite powerful and I began my journey of relating differently to my story. Some practitioners specialized in Psych-K, reprogramming subconscious beliefs, family constellation therapy for dealing with family and ancestral entanglement, and somatic bodywork, which emphasizes internal, physical perception and experiencing. There were many other modalities and therapies that I'm eternally grateful for. I naturally learned how to do or became certified in the methods that seemed to work, and I brought them into my practice.

I found it fascinating that my bodywork practice, which I gave the name Goodbye Tension, naturally brought me clients who also had some form of trauma that needed to be processed. They were naturally releasing as I was doing bodywork with them. So, the skills I was learning to heal myself were the same skills that I was using to guide others. I realized that many people had some sort of traumatic or adverse life experience in their life. The word "trauma" feels like a very charged word; the reality is, any experience that we've had that wasn't easily digestible is considered adverse. As long as we don't judge it as being greater than or less than something else, the label doesn't matter so much. The reality is that undigestible experiences are a form of trauma that has left an impression in the mind-body system.

With my weight loss journey, I learned about gut digestion, different foods that would increase or reduce weight, different types of exercise, etc. I was learning about mental and emotional digestion through the processing of various kinds. Little did I know this was all leading toward a doctorate some years later. When I write about my journey, I can see all the blessings in each moment. Me learning to love myself also came from working with others and realizing lack of self-love is a bigger universal problem. Most people don't have a good relationship with themselves for one reason or another, and if all the relationships we form in our lives are based on how well we first know ourselves, then this was something that needed radical change. If you recall earlier, I referenced how change was a triggering feeling, a triggering thought, a triggering word; it triggered excitement and fear. Since there had been so much fear in my life, the first experience held within my mind-body was fear.

As I worked with clients, I got to see other people's fear, how it froze them, and I could self-reference my own experience. Somehow, observing it and experiencing it from the perspective of the practitioner sped up my recovery. I could see how each client trusted me, and, many times, I felt my clients trusted me more than I even knew how to trust myself. Their trust in me gave me confidence that something came through even though I wasn't directly aware of it. My ability to hold space when somebody had an emotional response, to create a safety net so that all reactions were accepted would become my thriving superpower. I didn't know it yet. As my practice grew, I continued healing. Finding courage in places, I had so much fear, and each step toward change brought more clients who needed that kind of guidance. I was continually motivating myself to elevate because people depended on my support. One of the commitments I made in my practice, probably within the first few years, was that I wanted a more conscious healing approach. I wanted to be different from the other practitioners around me by creating an environment and offering services that got to the core of the problem. Each modality, method, or process that I learned or became certified in and offered all had that same approach.

I started to get excited about being triggered. I know that sounds crazy, and at some point, you may get excited about it as well. Even as I write these words, I'm chuckling within myself as the tears hit the page because triggers had dominated every aspect of my being. My fears and triggers determined every action I took in my life. When a trigger comes, I get excited, most of the time, because I'm headed toward an upgrade as long as I'm willing to face it and no longer controlled by this unconscious force, belief, and impression.

When I think about where I was vs. where I am now, I'm incredibly humbled and grateful. You see, our triggers are pointing out that which is already within. Whoever has evoked the trigger is the gift that has been offered, pointed out to you. It's no different than having somebody point out that you have mustard on your face; it's already there. But what tends to happen is more of a reaction to the person or event that's pointing out the trigger, which is where we begin the avoidance method. Why? Because it's painful. Sometimes that trigger is so sad because it's pointing to a deeper wound. In my case, those deeper wounds were so intense that I feared a breakdown. Considering that there's a history in the familial line of mental disease, and some generations were committed to an asylum, I was genuinely worried that my breakdown might lead to that. It didn't help that the professionals whom I was seeking help from, in the beginning, couldn't handle it either. Yet, somehow, that inner voice continued to cheer me on. I had an unusual amount of faith that I can do this, and it's going to be challenging.

I wanted something different for myself. I wanted something different for my children. I wanted something different for my children's children, and so on. So, I learned that my breakdowns were breakthroughs, but I had to ride the wave.

I call these storms. Do you know where the safest place is in a storm? It's in the center. Think of a hurricane. The calmest place of a storm is the eye, meaning, you stay stable at that one point as the storm is happening around you. I often use this visual for myself and my clients because when one is emotionally processing, a lot is going on. It's easy to step out of that eye and get caught up in the storm and be taken on quite an intense ride that thrashes you about and spits you out somewhere later. But learning to stay in the eye of the storm allows you to watch it like a movie while still having emotional responses and feelings as that movie is playing. Some of the Kriya practices that I learned, Tai Chi and Yoga, helped me focus on a single point while navigating my storms.

When you begin this type of healing, having a practitioner capable of holding space and guiding you through these moments and suggesting the appropriate variety of breathwork, focus/meditative process, and lifestyle adjustments is a must.

Now the blessing of having come from and healing so much trauma, so far, is that I feel that anyone who walks through my door looking for help, I'll have the tools to help them. I also have the tools and awareness to realize when I don't have the capacity, and I then refer out to a more appropriate practitioner. In the 18 years that I've been in practice, I haven't heard anything that was more than I could handle, and this also has given me the confidence to hold space, no matter what I hear.

My healing journey has been and continues to be precisely what most people are needing. Each client that comes in is an opportunity for growth. I learn so much and continue to from each client. I realized early on in my practice that I could only guide others up to the point at which I had healed myself. That type of mentality and understanding means that continual growth and change would need to happen. That's what has been happening. Since I began the more in-depth healing process, I found it quite fascinating the level of compassion I could have for others, yet there were still places where I wasn't very compassionate with myself. At times, I felt like an imposter in these situations. Yet another judgment waiting to be witnessed and questioned. Here I was guiding others toward being compassionate with themselves, and I hadn't figured it out yet. I accept that I'm human and not looking for perfection, just growth. The first step is being able to see it. Only when we're willing to see ourselves as we are and where we are can we begin to change.

We're all on this journey together. I make it a point to let my clients know I'm not perfect. I'm still a work in progress. I'm not a psychologist. My life experience, professional certifications, training, and the degree that I'm currently in process with as a Doctor of Ayurveda, with a specialty in the Mind known as Sattvavajaya Chikitsa are what allow me to help others.

What if mental health is being comfortable enough in our body that we don't need to numb ourselves or escape from our feelings
-Edan Harari

 Have courage to begin, commitment to stick with it, and an openness to change.

 You can only begin a journey from where you are.

Chapter 5

Changing How I Relate with My Story

I certainly didn't want to be in a victim mindset, which is easy to do when it comes to trauma. Please understand that statement. Coming out of a victim mindset doesn't excuse the behavior of those who committed harm against you. Being in a victim mindset felt disempowering, so I changed how I was relating to my story. I wanted to feel empowered, which meant I needed to change how I was associating with my story. I set out to be the master of myself.

Since my trauma was the first 25 years of my life, I set out to heal those parts of myself during that timeframe. I certainly didn't have to go looking for what to heal as I knew a trigger would come soon enough to point out what needed attention. When a trigger of being rejected came up in my friendships, I would take a journey inward-looking for the part of me that was afraid. This was the beginning of changing the victim mindset and relating to my story vs. feeling like a victim who was rejected. That exploration led to discovering a little girl I would later realize was my inner child. This fearful little one (I call her "Lil J"), about four years old, was sitting alone in a house, wondering where her parents were. She felt abandoned by them, and that feeling was manifesting in my adult relationships. It was clear that this "Lil J" needed healing and I wanted to take full responsibility for "Lil J" so that she wasn't at the mercy of others. In this particular healing, I could see that "Lil J" needed the security of Mother and Father who stayed and nurtured her and didn't leave her alone at four years old. I decided to take responsibility for "Lil J" by bringing in the aspect of me that could be the loving, nurturing Mother and Father.

These aspects of Mother and Father, originating from a larger, higher, resolved place of my being, came in and gave "Lil J" precisely what she needed. They also committed to never leave her alone until she was grown enough for that phase of life. This commitment is probably the most important in the healing phase of this type of inner child work. The reason being, I disconnected from myself at four years old during a moment of the intense fear of abandonment. The disconnect happened due to the inability to process and digest mentally and emotionally what was happening. As I grew up, my four-year-old aspect was stuck in a time loop of trauma. The loop was activated when I was in relation with others and felt alone, rejected, abandoned, or perceived the possibility of abandonment, which also meant that I was projecting this possibility in my relationships. My fear of abandonment led to my abandoning behavior in relationships, trying to prevent being hurt. In my efforts to not be hurt, I hurt others. Wounded people wound others when their wounds aren't tended to.

To heal this time loop, I had to come in and first acknowledge "Lil J," see what she needed, take full responsibility for her by embodying the Mother and Father role for her, which included the commitment not to abandon. In this way, I was building trust with "Lil J" so that she would come into integration with the rest of me and no longer be in a state of disconnect. As the integration happened, I began relating to others differently. My experiences of rejection and abandonment shifted. I was getting to know myself as a new upgraded version of me, and so were others. The relationship with myself had improved, and, naturally, relationships improved with others. I was now relating differently to "My story."

The realization of the profound impacts of the inner child healing led me to create the EDHIR® process. The acronym EDHIR®:Explore, Discover, Heal, Integrate, and Relate. The process that allows you to be true to yourself. I'll discuss this in more detail in the next chapter.

As I explored, I discovered many different versions of my inner child at different ages and moments in time that were on repeating time loops. Every time I got triggered, a different version of a disconnected inner-child aspect of myself would start reliving that moment of trauma. Once I became aware through the Explore and Discover phase, I could Heal these aspects. What I discovered was that "Lil J" was very afraid and alone. Most of the time, these different aspects needed Mother and Father love. I learned to become my own Mother, Father, etc. My inner child needed an unconditionally loving mother and father with no hidden agenda or expectation. The Blueprint I came into this world with wasn't going to give me that. I had to learn it for myself. I found this to be a little challenging, since every time I saw the younger versions of me, I got triggered by seeing the innocence that reminded me of what was lost. So, I remembered what I learned about being in the eye of the storm, watching it like a movie.

With each discovery, I was rewriting my story, the little girl, who had been physically, mentally, emotionally, psychologically, and sexually abused for so long; I started giving her what she needed in the moments before those abuses happened. I came in as the appropriate mother or appropriate father, depending on what she needed. The experience of the inner child was changed, changing the traumatic impressions into positive and healthy impressions. I didn't have to go through every grueling memory, thank goodness! I discovered that if I could go to some of the youngest moments, that would change the timeline of my perception in my psyche. In other words, if the very first memory of abuse didn't leave an impression, according to my perception in my mind, then events that had come after that would practically be healed, or at least that's my theory. This doesn't take away the actual occurrence of abuse; it starts the process of a new impression so that the relationship with that part of the story is different.

For example, by becoming mother and father to my inner child, I have much more trust because I'm receiving the new impressions this way. My inner child is learning to become self-sufficient from that wholesome mother/father love, instead of feeling disconnected and alone, needing the mother/father love from the old impression of mother/father.

As I learned how to become my mother and my father, I became a better mother myself. I became a better father to my children, who didn't have a father yet. I noticed that the relationships around me started changing. In the healing work that I do with clients, I reference weeding your garden. What happens as you heal, you become upgraded, and sometimes the relationships around you will change, the equivalent to your garden needing to be cleared out for something new. Not all flowers and herbs are meant to be together, and, at some point, they may need to be put in a different garden.

As individual relationships started changing, new flowers (friends and well-wishers) were brought into the garden while others naturally decayed, allowing for more space, the equivalent of boundaries.

Boundaries aren't usually something that someone who has been abused learns very well because, at a very young age, boundaries were violated whenever trauma happened; therefore, the understanding of boundaries doesn't quite compute. The relationships I attracted into my life or let go of resulted from the healing that I was doing. However, it wasn't just the healing; it was also integrating. So, as I healed more aspects of my inner child, I was becoming more whole. These aspects were no longer disconnected. They had been given the love, support, and healing they needed to join me in this journey and not be operating as a disconnect outside of me, on autopilot, getting triggered and retriggered, etc. The quality of relationships in my life changed to more mature, interdependent relationships.

As I became more whole, I was also guiding others toward becoming more whole. The more I got to know myself, the more I realized I'm pretty cool, and others think so too. It took a while for me to get here and see that I learned to take my negative experiences and, with awareness, turn them into a positive.

The emotional baggage was turned into a massive bag of experiences and tools.

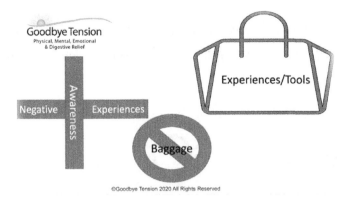

The more I worked on myself, the better my brain started working, and I realized that anything is possible because I believe in myself and am less reliant on needing validation from others. Within me, I can give myself the mothering; I can give myself the fathering, I can be my best husband or best wife depending on what I need, my best friend, etc.

Looking at many of the world's problems that have gone on historically, most issues are based on an inability to relate. How on earth will we possibly have a healthy world when we don't even know how to connect with ourselves most of the time. How can we create a healthy family environment? How do we create healthy communities if the family units aren't healthy? Once the communities are healthy, the communities go out, and the world can be healthy. If we were truly connected healthily with ourselves and each other, would Mother Earth be the way that she is? We've lost our ability to relate with her because of our unhealthy inner relationship.

If you love yourself, you love others. If you hate yourself, you hate others. In relationships with others, it is only you, mirrored.

-Osho

 Healing doesn't take away the actual occurrence of abuse; it starts the process of a new impression so that the relationship with that part of the story is different.

 Negative experiences with awareness become a positive.

 Turn your emotional baggage into a large bag of tools and experience.

Chapter 6

The EDHIR® Process

Adhere: **Pronunciation** /əd'hir/ /əd'hɪr/

Defined: to believe in and follow the practices of; to represent truthfully and in detail.[1]

EXPLORE PHASE: Step 1

---

1   https://www.lexico.com/en/definition/adhere

Are you satisfied with who you are?

Are you satisfied with your relationships?

Do you feel stuck or blocked in some aspect of your life?

Do you have trauma or experiences that keep replaying in your thoughts and dreams?

These are just a few questions that will deepen the exploratory phase.

Maybe you notice a theme in your life that keeps repeating, or perhaps you have physical discomfort or, even worse, a disease.

The idea here's to dive deeper on an exploratory mission to see what you discover.

We begin the exploratory phase by first connecting with the breath.

Inhale quickly, through your nose, to the count of 4 as the belly rises and then exhale slowly to the count of 8 by pursing the lips as the belly lowers. This is one Deep Diaphragmatic Breath.[2]

Find a comfortable place to sit, with your feet on the ground and ideally the spine is straight; begin with 1 minute of deep diaphragmatic breathing. Once you feel you understand how to do the breathing, you can close your eyes.

As you close your eyes, this will allow you to go inward into the uniqueness of your being. Continue to follow the breath in and out at a slow and relaxed pace. You only need to focus on the in and out of your breath. The

---

2   https://youtu.be/3SAzl_MmlsE

mind may have its thoughts, and it will be tempting to follow the thoughts. Do your best to follow your breath as this is the most crucial step; you're preparing the system for a journey.

Wherever the breath goes, the mind follows, meaning a slow, relaxed breath, especially on the exhale will allow the body, mind, and heart to be open and expanded vs. closed off. Narrow vision—if you've ever had an anxious moment, you know what I'm referring to—is tunnel vision and an inability to see and sense clearly with a rapid breathing pattern and an abundance of fast-moving thoughts running through the mind. This breath practice is also creating more awareness within you. The most powerful tool we have is our breath, and it's also the most forgotten.

Now we need to connect to the body. Remember, an adverse experience is stored somewhere within you, and sometimes the experience is so intense that one may leave the body out of fear. Being connected and rooted is a must before we start this exploration.

As you continue with your eyes closed, following the deep breathing pattern, wiggle your toes and feel them on the ground. Feel your toes, and now feel your breath and awareness in your toes. Feel your heels and the bottom of your feet; bring the next breath and attention to the feet. Follow this pattern to the lower leg, back and front side (calf and shin area); breathe deeply and bring your awareness here. You're moving up now to the knees, both the backside and the front; take a deep breath as you become aware of your knees. Breathe deeply and bring awareness to your thighs, the backside on the seat, and the front side where your hands may naturally be resting. As you continue to follow your breath in and out, you notice your seat and pelvic area; do a squeeze here. For women, this is the equivalent of a Kegel squeeze, and for men it's the type of contraction you would do if you needed to hold back your urine or gas.

DON'T SKIP THE SQUEEZE!

The squeeze is bringing awareness to your root. When you go deeper into these five phases, remember the squeeze combined with the breath to calm you and ground you.

Now bring your deep belly breath into your abdomen and lower back as you become aware of this space. Sometimes, this can be a challenging place to connect with for many reasons. If this is you, place your right hand on your lower abdomen and the left hand on the low back to give the body the touch signal, which can create awareness. Take another breath here.

Moving your awareness now to the belly button and midback, feel the belly rise and fall as you stay here for another breath. As you bring your awareness and breath upward to the rib cage, feel your lungs fill up as much as possible, feeling the expansion in the front, sides, and back of your ribs and lungs.

Take another deep belly breath as you bring your awareness to your heart space. Try to feel the sensation in the front of the heart and the back of the heart. Maintain awareness in the heart space. Continue to follow your breath, bring attention to your shoulders, down to your elbows, wrists, hands, and fingers. Wiggle your fingers with the next breath and follow the inhale up to the throat, the place where you speak your truth.

Now bring your awareness and your deep breath to the back of your skull. Up around to the top of your head, feeling the oxygen fill your brain, and then exhale. Relax your forehead and feel your eyes sink back into the sockets. Bring awareness and the next breath to your jaw. Wiggle your jaw and relax. Breathe deeply from the top of your head down to the tips of your toes back and forth. Now that the body and mind are more relaxed with the breath flowing with a nice slow rhythm, we'll begin exploring.

If you already brought an idea or an issue, then that's what you'll explore. For example, I'm going to bring the feeling of being scared. As I explore the sensation of being afraid, I notice my tummy has butterflies and nervousness. My heart is fluttering. My breath is starting to speed up. I remember the breath and do the deep diaphragmatic breathing again so that the breath is at a relaxed pace. What I'm exploring is the earliest memory of fear. I'm exploring the possibility of finding the earliest version of me stuck in time and afraid.

Why the earliest version or earliest memory? If healing can happen for the earliest memory, the entire timeline changes. That doesn't mean that the situation that created the fear didn't happen. In my mind, the impression has been loosened and can now move and be digested. I'm no longer so viscerally impacted by the sensation and feeling of fear.

I see a very young version of myself in the dark, about three years old, dark circles under her eyes. Her hair hasn't been washed or brushed. Her eyes are big and filled with fear. I notice how sharp her teeth seem. I look around to see if there are any other signs or symbols that stand out in my exploration. And I notice the baby blanket all torn and dirty, lying on the floor. This particular blanket happened to be the one I grew up with; that was a safety blanket. I notice that she has her back toward me, which represented that she's unaware of my presence or not ready to see me. I need to be very careful in how I approached her to help her sense me. If she were at a side profile, she would have some awareness of me. And if she were directly facing me, she would be aware of my presence and ready to be seen. But in this particular healing, I needed to help her become aware of my presence so that we could discover what was needed to heal.

DISCOVERY PHASE: Step 2

You'll now discover what's happening. Try to be open and not judge what you see, as all discoveries are acceptable. There's a part of you with a message. Once you discover the news, you'll be able to offer healing and change.

I discovered this aspect of myself, and now I needed to find out what the story was and how to get her to sense my presence and trust me.

So how was I going to do this? There were signs of neglect and fear. Her teeth's sharpness gave great detail of how long she may have been here, reliving this particular trauma. It had taken its toll as she had a savageness to her. I could see that she needed a bath, new clothes, a washed and mended blanket, as well as someone whom she could trust that would take care of her.

HEALING PHASE: Step 3

You'll now offer that version of yourself everything needed to come out of the trauma time loop.

I decided to get down on my knees to be more at her height level. Standing above or over her would have made her feel threatened. I very softly said hello and patiently waited for a response. She responded, startled, and glanced over her shoulder as we exchanged a glance. "It is okay, little one. I'm not going to hurt you," I said. The facial expression told me that she didn't believe what I was saying. I knew that I was going to have to try something different. I brought in some small toys to the situation and started playing with them on the floor, waiting to see if she would respond to this. I noticed that her body started turning more in my direction; this was a good sign. As I played with the toys, I slowly moved the toys closer toward her as an invitation. *Maybe she would be curious enough to come and play*, I thought. She grabbed her tattered blanket and came closer. She grabbed the teddy bear then pulled herself away quickly as if expecting a harsh reaction from me. I told her she could have the teddy bear. It was my gift to her with no expectation in return. I told her how beautiful her blanket was, and she smirked. As I expressed how smart she was, I explained that I wanted to help her. I said, "I understand that others who've tried to offer help before had other intentions in mind. I'm you all grown up, and I want you to be a part of me so we can grow up together." She looked deep into my eyes, and I could see that she wanted to believe me. "It seems dark in here. Maybe we could take a walk toward the sun?" I asked. Her eyes looked around the room. I started walking in the direction of sunlight, inviting her to join me. But she wasn't sure. I got as far as the edge of the dark room, just enough so the light could start peering in. I brought in a beautiful clean set of clothes, a sewing machine to mend her blanket, and a nice warm bowl of water with a washcloth so that we could wash the dirt off. She liked the outfit as It was a beautiful blue dress. She wanted to put it on. I asked her if it would be okay to wash her first in a very safe and loving way. She could change her mind at any point. So, as I began washing this little one. I was telling her how special she is and the life that's ahead of her. I promised that I was never going to leave her behind. She slipped into her beautiful blue dress, admiring the frills of the hem. She began to smile, handed me her blanket, which I washed, and mended. I asked her if she'd like to go for a walk in her beautiful blue dress, giving her the option to come back to the dark, cold room that she had learned to feel safe in at any time. I reached out my left hand toward her, and she reached out her right. Holding hands, we walked out into the sun into a beautiful field with wildflowers and lots of space. She let go of my hand and ran all through the area, happy and skipping.

Before moving to the Integration phase of the process, the healing needs to feel complete. I needed to be sure that this version of me trusted me, felt loved and nurtured, and felt safe with this particular situation. I would need a sign, and I decided that the sharp teeth would be the sign. Once the teeth changed, integration could begin. If I didn't wait for this sign, I risked creating harm to myself as there could be resistance and a fight within my mind if the trust weren't first established.

To clarify, this is all me. I refer to the three-year-old as her-separate from me before we come into integration.

Meanwhile, she ran and skipped out in the field of wildflowers. At different times she would look back to see if I were still there. Eventually, she got tired and laid down to rest. As I approached her, I asked her if she was ready to close the door to the dark room she learned to live in. Of course, she is about three years old, so I was doing my best to communicate at that level. She was confused a bit and ran, scared, back to the dark room. I followed her, crawling on my knees so that I was more on her level and not intimidating or inciting more fear. The room had already started shifting because she had a taste of trust and daylight. I could see windows now that were dirty, so I went over and opened one of them so that she could have more light. She looked around, confused. All that was so familiar (and completely inappropriate) had changed enough that she felt a bit of unease mixed with hope. I started cleaning the room, and each time she smiled, her teeth were looking better and better. Once it was all clean, I promised her that we would live together, and I would never hurt her or abandon her.

Whatever abuse had happened at that age was too much to handle, and I disconnected from myself during the process, essentially abandoning a part of me to survive. This is a self-preservation mechanism that many abuse survivors can relate to; however, it can happen in any experience that was too much to handle. Remember the two-year-old little boy who drew such a beautiful picture for his mom and then felt so rejected by her when she didn't acknowledge him because she was busy cooking dinner? He wasn't abused; however, he had an experience that left an impression where it was too much to handle, so he left that version behind, reliving the wound in all his relationships.

Now that the three-year-old version of me was healing, we could begin the integration phase.

INTEGRATION PHASE: Step 4

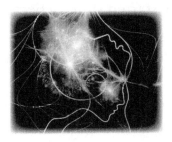

Integration is combining and coordinating separate parts or elements into a unified whole. Now the fun begins. An upgrade is about to happen.

I explored the feeling of fear and discovered a three-year-old version of myself that needed healing, and now we are ready to come together and integrate into a united whole.

The integration phase begins once this three-year-old version agrees to leave the current time loop and trusts me to take responsibility for her. Once I cleaned up that dark room, committed never to leave her, and showed her the opposite experience to the one she was stuck in, she was ready and hopeful for what was next. She agreed to leave with me, and we walked out into the field, holding hands as she grew older and began connecting from that moment. As we walked, our hands blended, and we slowly integrated and became one.

Returning to the present moment

The same way you relaxed the body using breath and awareness in the beginning is the same way you come out of this healing session.

Come out very slowly as you're not the same person as you were going in, and you may feel disoriented.

I began connecting with my breath, wiggling my toes, feeling my feet, legs, hips, pelvic squeeze, and following the breath with awareness from the tips of my toes to the top of my head, and slowly began opening my eyes.

It's essential to identify three things, preferably living, such as plants, in the current space so that all of you has returned from the healing journey inward.

I identified the plants outside my window, another indoor plant, and the water in my cup. As I stayed connected with my breath, I didn't speak for about 5 minutes because I was trying to acclimate to the new upgraded version of myself, as I certainly felt different.

RELATE PHASE: Step 5

Now is where you get to date yourself. You have been upgraded, which will take some time for you to relate with yourself and with others.

For some, the change is noticeable immediately, but for others, it's subtle. Either experience is excellent. Remember, we aren't judging any of it; allow openness and willingness to evolve.

As I got to know myself after this upgrade, the most significant signs were my responses to moments that would have customarily evoked a fear response, which included fight, flight, and freeze. I even said WOW out loud in the middle of that moment, wondering why I wasn't triggered. I was inquisitive. I expected the trigger, and it didn't come, so I went looking for it, and it was nowhere to be found at that moment.

Other aspects of my life began to change because I had less fear; I communicated better and easily said yes to things I would have typically said no. I wasn't even aware of the part held back due to fear since the trigger had always been so intense it was usually about coping and managing. I was surviving, but now I was on my way to thriving.

My friends and family noticed a change, and, for the most part, this was an easy shift for them to relate. I did have a friend, though, with whom we had always connected with our trauma. Once I did this healing, we weren't relating in the same way.

Weeding your garden

We all have a garden that represents our internal and external lives. When changes happen, the garden may need some updating to allow for space to grow and blossom. Some plants and flowers that once grew well together are now suffocating and not able to grow together. Those flowers may need to be moved either further off in the garden or moved into a completely different garden. When you start changing, it can be a trigger for some of the people around you. Sometimes a feeling of insecurity may come up for others as it points out where they need to grow. A trigger is pointing out that which is already there within you. The person or event that's triggering is the blessing that has come, pointing out where you need to grow. Try to see these moments as an opportunity for growth and change. Love what comes and love what goes.

The friend with whom I was so close for ten years was going after I did my healing on the feeling of being afraid. I still loved her and completely understood where she was. She wasn't ready to look at what I was now triggering in her.

I should clarify that there are many aspects and faces of fear, and what I healed that day was a specific feeling of anxiety triggered by the belief that I would be betrayed . As the different faces of fear show up, the more healing has an opportunity to happen.

Many more versions of fear have shown up since then that I've been able to "EDHIR®" to the process. I still have many aspects of fear to be healed within me. The healing process is similar to an onion; there are many layers and tears, and the more you peel away, the closer you get to the "Heart" of the matter.

 Explore, Discover, Heal, Integrate and Relate is the process that allows you to be true to yourself.

 Make yourself a priority.

Chapter 7

Is Your Big Toe Triggered?

Now, this may sound silly; however, it works surprisingly well. I must give my husband, Ramiel, credit, as he asked me this very question in a triggered moment. The wisdom was so profound that I've been asking that question to clients and myself ever since.

How do you know what part of you is triggered, especially when the feeling has consumed you? Start asking yourself if certain body parts are triggered. The big toe is a great place to start because it gets you out of your mind. When my husband asked this, I burst out loud with laughter. Try it. Ask yourself, "Is my big toe triggered?" Once you have the answer, you can start asking more toes, fingers, limbs, etc.

This helps you relate with your trigger differently, becoming more of a witness to the trigger vs. reacting to the trigger. It will also bring awareness to the part of your body; that may have an impression that needs your attention.

Fill out the Trigger Worksheet Below:

TRIGGER WORKSHEET

Date: Time:

Describe Triggering Moment...

Where in your body do you feel this Trigger...?

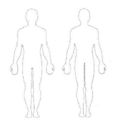

What are the feelings you're experiencing
from this trigger...?
(Refer to the feelings list.)
I feel....

Discover the exact moment you got triggered.

Word/Phrase:
Look:
Smell:
Person:
Body Language:
Other:

I'm Triggered by...

Follow steps 1-10 in the pocket guide located in the back of the book.

Goodbye Tension
Physical, Mental, Emotional
& Digestive Relief

Feelings List

Angry	Scared	Sad
Hate	Weak	Lonely
Mad	Rejected	Hurt
Furious	Helpless	Unhappy
Frustrated	Confused	Regretful
Irritated	Insecure	Down
Rage	Anxious	Depressed
Jealous	Discouraged	Miserable
Hostile	Embarrassed	Sorrow
Skeptical	Foolish	Rejected
Selfish	Submissive	Guilty
Hurt	Rejected	Inadequate
Critical	Insignificant	Inferior

Peace	Power	Joy
Loving	Safe	Happy
Calm	Valued	Delightful
Thoughtful	Appreciated	Excited
Relaxed	Confident	Playful
Nurturing	Intelligent	Energetic
Content	Respected	Creative
Undisturbed	Secure	Satisfied
Sentimental	Important	Radiant
Harmonious	Resilient	Blissful
Soothing	Positive	Hopeful
Thankful	Self-Reliant	Grateful
Pleasant	Assured	Fulfilled

The questioning is the Explore phase of EDHIR®, step one.

Once you discover which part of you is triggered, you have entered the Discover phase of EDHIR®; step two. Take a few deep breaths and close your eyes as you tune in to this part that's triggered. Can you identify the feeling? Is there a thought that arises? Is there a memory, or does the experience remind you of something or someone? Have you ever had this trigger before, and, if so, when was the earliest age you can remember about this type of trigger?

As you answer these questions, do your best to breathe deeply, and not get lost in this process. The discovery process is about trying to stay objective about what you're noticing needs to be healed, which means being aware of the feelings, thoughts, images, etc. without judgment. You may not always like what you discover. However, change can only happen once you're aware of where you are. If that is where you feel like you don't want to be a parent, for example, even though you have four kids, you may not want to become conscious of that feeling or thought. However, not acknowledging it means your thoughts, feelings, actions, etc. have this impression driving them, becoming destructive over time. For example, if your real sense is that you don't want to be in your role and choose to ignore it, your subconscious actions will come through with this intention even though you don't want to see it. Healing can only happen once you become aware of the dis-ease.

The questions you answer about the trigger allow you to discover more about the dis-ease you're experiencing.

Now that you have more information from your Exploration and Discovery, you can now move into the Healing phase of EDHIR®, step three.

Essentially, you want to try to give yourself the opposite quality of what you're feeling, and that can seem rather abstract at first.

There's a story that has developed from your Exploration and Discovery of your trigger. Imagine you're now hearing this story from the innocence of a child (any age; the idea is a moment of innocence, naiveness, immaturity, unawareness, etc. I was healing my inner-child up to age 25), and you want this child to feel loved, supported, seen, and understood so that they can grow up to be healthy and independent, not codependent.

Once you can see this story unravel from this child, you allow yourself to get big and embody the healthy archetype or guardian that this child needs for healing; this will depend on the story, of course. My experience is that the most common required archetypes are Mother and Father and others like brother, sister, teacher, husband, wife, etc.

At first, you may need to imagine what all the qualities are for these archetypes.

I knew from my upbringing what qualities I didn't want in a mother, father, and husband but wasn't sure what the positive, healthy traits were, so I explored and observed others in these roles in life, stories, movies, etc. When I first tried to "Get Big" and embody the healthy

Mother archetype, I wasn't able to connect it as being a part of me, so I imagined that it was a great evolved ancestor from thousands of years ago who was so pure and unconditionally loving.

The more I healed, the easier it became to connect with my inner mother guardian archetype to offer my inner child that healing. The same can be done for any archetype. I began looking up the opposite qualities of what I received growing up to find out what qualities a healthy mother archetype was needed for me. I needed boundaries, appropriate affection, presence, and strength in Mind and Heart along with trust. I suggest you research the qualities that embody the different archetypes that you can refer to when you're doing your inner healing work.

With each healing, there needs to be an integration between you and this part of you that was discovered and healed: EDHIR®, Step 4, Integration phase. This can happen in many ways. Once you've made your commitment, offering all that is needed for trust, then you can decide if you would like to go play with them or take a nice walk, etc. until you can see the two of you become one. Essentially, this integration will awaken parts of you that may have been forgotten or have never been known that were always there in the disconnected part of yourself. Then you move into the Relating phase of EDHIR®, Step five. This may take time, as all relationships do, to get to know yourself with this new integration. Keep an open mind and try not to have expectations. You are discovering a new version of yourself and that should be an exciting and curious time. This also means that the people around you may have to adjust as well.

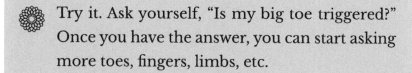 Try it. Ask yourself, "Is my big toe triggered?" Once you have the answer, you can start asking more toes, fingers, limbs, etc.

It helps to zoom in on which part is triggered, especially when your experience is that all of you is triggered.

I'm TRIGGERED! Now What!? Let's ask the big toe. ;-)

Now try working the EDHIR® steps.

Chapter 8

Let Your Triggers Be Your Teachers

The last thing you want to hear when you're triggered is that the person or event that triggered you is a blessing because it's pointing out that which is already inside you, which is an opportunity to apply the EDHIR® process to the trigger. Adhere means to be true to, as in be true to yourself.

Let your trigger show you what's been hiding within. Have courage and commitment to yourself. What if you've been subscribing to a lie and the trigger is trying to point out the lie? What if EDHIR® is your unsubscribe button?

Let's face it; You don't want to be triggered. Wouldn't you want to do anything to stop that experience? Wouldn't it be nice if that particular trigger stopped happening?

The only way to move forward is to be willing to see where you are.

You're triggered, have the courage and commitment to move forward, and not avoid yourself any longer.

Remember, the trigger is just pointing out that which has been inside you all along. It's a part of you, and avoiding it is no different than seeing you have an infected wound and pretending it doesn't exist. The wound continues to grow and fester and eventually leads to a more severe dis-ease. Doing the EDHIR® process is like pouring hydrogen peroxide on the wound, stitching it up, and bandaging it till it's healed. It stings at first but it's better than leaving it infected.

Imagine who you would be if you weren't triggered.

Try that now; make a list of who you would be or what it would be like if you weren't triggered.

Now take that list and post it everywhere in your home, computer screen, digital device, etc.; this will be your courage and commitment reminder to move forward and EDHIR® to your triggers.

Accountability

Accountability is super important. Find someone you trust to keep you accountable on your journey of courage and commitment toward maintaining loyalty to yourself by facing the illusion that your triggers create.

Let's begin by making a list of the people who trigger or irritate you.

Goodbye Tension
Physical, Mental, Emotional
& Digestive Relief

Known Triggers List

People:
1.
2.
3.

Places:
1.
2.
3.

Things:
1.
2.
3.

Behaviors:
1.
2.
3.

Other:
1.
2.
3.

What would it be like if I weren't triggered?

Who would I be without this trigger?

This list is a great starting place to actively work with the EDHIR® process.

Yes, I'm suggesting you go searching for your triggers to get used to working through this process. This way, muscle memory is more likely to kick in when you get sideswiped by a trigger.

The practice is the equivalent of studying before an exam. If you've run through enough simulations, you'll have a more extensive skill set when the real exam (trigger) happens.

The Perception of FEAR

I love to use the acronym Face Everything And Rise when I see the word "fear." This way, I'm essentially changing my relationship with fear.

The emotion of fear limits our ability to think, act, and perceive. That's not to say that the fear you experience when you face a life-threatening situation (i.e., a lion attacking you, a rapist, murderer) prevents you from thinking. That particular scenario and reaction keeps you alive. I'm referring to the perception of fear when there's no real danger; A trigger is fear. Thinking and acting from a triggered state is driven by fear.

The problem arises when we're unable to recognize when we're operating from a place of fear. The trigger is in the driver's seat, totally afraid and unable to think; this is where you need to call on your higher mind, higher heart, higher self, higher power, etc. The basic principle is to elevate from the triggered place. The first step to coming out of fear is acknowledging that you're in a fearful state, and you need wisdom. Fear is the belief in something outside of yourself. Never forget your fearless self. The courageous and committed aspect of you that doesn't run away from fear or fight with fear, but faces what you're afraid of; looking at it directly and discovering what's true.

The nature of the mind is continuous movement. Imagine you're in your favorite country and now your least favorite place. Now try not to think of either place. You see, in a split second, you could be in India and the next in Europe and then both. Unless you train the mind, its nature is to be anywhere and everywhere. If you train your mind to face its fears, you'll be utilizing your mind's sole purpose as a tool to use, not something that uses you.

PERCEPTION

Perception is how we interpret the input we're ingesting through our senses. How we interpret what we saw and what we felt becomes our perception. We hear, smell, taste, and analyze everything, which is how we perceive it.

Let's say you went on a late evening walk with a friend and noticed something on the ground in front of you. Your friend perceives it as a stick, while you perceive it as a snake. Since it's dark, you wouldn't know who was correct until more light or awareness came to the situation. This object, perceived as fear from one perspective and logic from another. As you grab your cell phone and turn on the flashlight, you see a stick. This object triggered the fear that was already inside. When you introduce light to dispel darkness or wisdom to dispel ignorance, the fear is observed as an imbalance in perception. Why did your friend have a logical response to the stick while you perceived it as a snake? Perhaps you were bitten by a snake when as a child you grabbed a stick from a wood pile. So, seeing a stick is a trigger for fear. Remember, fear limits and sometimes paralyzes your ability to think and act. The rational and objective part of the mind doesn't function properly because fear has taken over. Whereas the one who naturally perceived the stick as a stick didn't have an underlying fear trigger and, therefore, could use logic, reason, and deduction to assess that it was a stick.

 Face Everything And Rise by allowing your triggers to be your teacher and using accountability with the perception of fear.

 If you train your mind to face its fears, you'll be utilizing your mind's sole purpose as a tool to use, not something that uses you.

Chapter 9

BREAKDOWN to BREAKTHROUGH

The words we use possess energy; I'm always listening to what words others and myself are saying. I feel it's best to use the phrase Breakthrough instead of Breakdown. Why? Breakdown reminds me of what happens when your car stops working and needs to be fixed. A Breakthrough feels as if there's something on the other side you're about to discover. Doesn't that feel much more uplifting than needing to be fixed? I often feel like a rock layer is being chiseled away when I'm working through a trigger. Once the chiseling is complete, I break through to a beautiful discovery of myself, a gift waiting to reveal itself. This is the motivation when you're at that fork in the road of fight, flight, or freeze. What if you stayed and started chiseling? At the very least, you would be trying something other than the usual trauma response that you've become accustomed to. At best, you find the gift that's waiting to be revealed. If you can remember this during your most challenging times, you'll have outstanding success in your process.

Now you may be thinking, *If I work on (fill in the blank), I'm afraid It will be too much, and I'll break down and never get up again.*

I get it, and I believed this for a long time myself. I decided to question this belief because it prevented me from moving forward in so many aspects of my life. I used The Work by Byron Katie. I used part of her method by asking myself, "Is it true that I'll break down if I face _____?"

My response was, "Well, it's a possibility....." I went to the next question.

"How do I know for certain it's true?" Darn, I couldn't say for sure it was true. Now I needed to answer how it made me feel when I believed that I would break down. I felt terrified and defeated by this belief. The final question, who would I be without this thought? I wouldn't be afraid or defeated; I noticed that I felt stronger when I stopped believing that I would break down. So, I realized how much power this thought had over me and decided to cancel my subscription to that belief. I've been breaking through ever since.

WHAT IF...

The most common fear-based thought, responsible for anxiety, distress, and the inability to move forward in life, is negative What if thoughts. The fear of what could happen is quite common for anyone with trauma. I remember staying up into the wee hours of the morning thinking of all the what if scenarios and how I would respond to them. The thoughts ranged from the snarky remark by someone with my witty response to driving on a bridge that collapses and how quickly I could jump out of the car before the car hit the water. Then there were the numerous bodily harm scenarios and my defense; this took up so much mind space and energy. It was quite exhausting, yet in my mind, I was preparing myself for all possibilities. Since I had experienced it in my mind, I would remember doing it should the event happen. Stephen Covey wrote, "All things are created twice. Before we act, we should act in our minds first." I was using this principle but in a negative way that wasn't supportive of who I wanted to be; where positive What if thoughts become my default.

Goodbye Tension
Physical, Mental, Emotional
& Digestive Relief

What If Worksheet

Date:

What if...

Does this statement imply fear or endless possibilities?

(Refer to the positive/negative words list and feelings list)

Rewrite the statement from fear to endless possibilities.

Example: What if I don't succeed? Implies fear.
What if I'm successful? Implies endless possibilities.

Based on your responses to the What if worksheet, you can see which side of the fence you're on, the fear side or the endless possibilities side. Both sides have an incredible amount of strength. The question is, are you where you want to be? Do you want to be on the fear side? Of course, you don't, and maybe it's all you've ever known. But what if on the other side there were endless possibilities that motivate and excite you about your life?

Go back to your worksheet and replace the negative, fear-based responses with a positive, motivating, continuous possibility response.

Take the first what if and consider its endless possibility. How do you feel? Are you still on the fear side, or are you moving to the endless possibility side?

The idea is to change the thought pattern from negative to positive. For example, if the negative thought is *Why do I even try?*, the positive thought could be I *wonder what new things I'll learn today from trying?* I prefer phrases that come from curiosity, so that I am open to all possibilities.

The positive phrase could become your daily affirmation or mantra.

A mind is a tool that you use. As with any tool, it needs to be cleaned, sharpened, polished, etc. Otherwise, it becomes corroded and dull. This practice is cleaning up the corrosion.

SURVIVING to THRIVING

Surviving[1] is to continue to live or exist, especially in spite of danger or hardship.

Thriving[2] is to prosper, be fortunate or successful, to grow or develop vigorously; flourish.

I started my new life with my daughters, continuously planning for the worst and hoping for the best, looking over my shoulder for the next traumatizing What if event that could happen. I was worried about making enough money, having time to help with the school work, and fig-

---

1   https://www.wordnik.com/words/surviving
2   https://www.wordnik.com/words/thriving

uring out how to get a divorce without an attorney, etc.; that was surviving. It was certainly better than the previous life, but it was far from thriving. My fear of What ifs were driving me. I needed a different mindset and more belief in myself, in life, and people; this is a crucial point. When I examined my relationships, they were mostly survivors, not thrivers. My environment internally and externally was supporting the survivor mindset. I needed to change my internal and external environment to support a thriving mindset.

I'm always fascinated by how the internal and external environments reflect each other. Being in a survival mindset led me to outer relationships that were also surviving. Like attracts like; so, I started looking for the opposite of what I was used to. I tried to go in the opposite direction of the friends I was naturally attracted to.

I want you to move from surviving to thriving!

If you were thriving, what would that look like for you?

It can get a little tricky, since those in a surviving mindset know that it's an improvement from being in the traumatic event and can't even imagine what thriving would be like. To thrive is to be on the endless possibilities side. Sure, you survived the trauma and are functioning as best as you know how. What if you were thriving, prospering, making steady progress, and believing in yourself?

My mission in life is not merely to survive, but to thrive; and to do so with some passion, some compassion, some humor, and some style.

—Maya Angelou

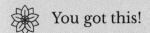 What if your breakdown turned into a breakthrough and you went from surviving to thriving?

You got this!

I believe in you and it's time you start believing in yourself.

Chapter 10

Being at Home Within Myself-Creating the Environment for Healing

By creating a sense of home internally, not only are you developing a relationship with yourself but you're also making a safe space within. For those who, while growing up, had unsafe homes or lived where there was no sense of individuality or boundaries, this is essential to the healing process. This is where you learn to trust yourself, provide for yourself, and take absolute full responsibility for yourself, including your happiness. It takes the dependency on others to make you happy off the table, creating space for interdependent relationships. Being at home creates a stable internal environment that you're the master of. As you evolve with this concept, you'll notice that no matter what the external circumstance, inside, you're safe, secure, and positive.

Your ability to see clearly in times of chaos comes from the internal stability of being at home within.

How often do you try to fill up your day with to-dos? Since I'm writing this book during COVID-19, this pandemic has created trauma and adverse life experiences for many. Suddenly, our to-do list in regards to leaving our home became very limited. And we had no choice but to stay home with ourselves and our spouse or partner, children, family, etc. The ability to feel a sense of home within yourself is one of the most powerful tools I've ever learned. The credit for this concept goes to my husband, Ramiel.

When you have a sense of home within yourself, it doesn't matter where you live. It doesn't matter whom you live with. It doesn't matter whom you know. You always feel safe within yourself. The better sense of home you have within yourself, the higher quality of relationships you'll attract into your life because you won't be coming from a place of need.

When I began the practice of learning how to be at home with myself, the feeling of anxiety increased to such a level that I thought I would pass out. Looking back, I can see just how out of balance I was and how incredibly scared I was; I had done so much running that my inner dialogue was all about running and leaving. There was no space to tune-in and check-in with the deeper aspects of myself; this is why dating yourself is so important.

Getting to know yourself when you're alone is profound. I would start by taking a day when I didn't interact with anyone else. I noticed my breathing would change;

I felt a sense of panic. What should I do? Should I try to write? When I would try to write, my mind would wander. Then, of course, social media was a vast distracter, and you have to be committed to not opening up the phone when you're getting to know yourself or having that alone time. Essentially, avoid anything that takes you away from that uncomfortable feeling that you're having when you're alone with yourself.

Fear not! This will change the more you do it. So, I used the panic feeling as a sign. And I tried to find the opposite quality. So, since there was panic, I thought to myself, *If a client of mine were coming with this feeling, what would I do to help them?*

I would try to create some nourishment and support. So, I needed to figure out how to do that for myself. I connected with my breath. Sometimes, all I could do was breathe and acknowledge, "I'm in a fearful state; this is how I'm relating with myself, and I'm going to breathe." I found the ocean as a very therapeutic place to be. I would often go to the beach or visualize I was at the beach. I would imagine my feelings, and every time I exhaled, the feelings would go out into the sea. I used the sound of the water and the waves to relax. And then I would close my eyes so that I turned inward to keep an eye on my breath. As the breath started to calm down, the heart rate would calm down.

Then I could be with this awareness that I'm scared. I'm afraid to be alone. I would turn on the video of my phone and start talking to myself to go back and reference what I observed. I began to see myself terrified. I could see this scared little girl in this adult woman's eyes that I was watching in this video. I needed to nurture her so that she wasn't so frightened. I healed and worked on myself; I realized my neediness in relationships was reducing. Each week, I would try to find a chunk of time when I could be with myself and notice whether or not I felt safe, a sense of home.

Of course, a sense of home, for me, was always a scary place. So, I didn't know how to create a sense of home within myself. I hadn't experienced all the foundations of what a healthy, functional family would typically bring to a child. I experienced the opposite. Again, I knew what I didn't want, but I needed to figure out what I wanted. I truly wanted to feel safe within myself without the need for a partner, without the need for children, and without the need for friends because I needed to learn how to trust myself first. So, this practice of feeling at home within myself has been ongoing. I'm now at a point where I can be anywhere with anyone. And I feel at home within myself. That doesn't mean I don't get triggered anymore; to be clear, it means that I'm at home within and aware that a trigger is happening. I'm aware that this trigger is happening within my inner home; it's an opportunity to turn on the lights to clean up whatever has triggered me.

Now when you think of creating your home, of course, there's furniture, lighting, aesthetics, pictures, etc. The same thing happens when you're finding a sense of home within yourself. That means no matter what the external circumstances are within you, you feel safe and supported, have a place to sleep, and have the nourishment that you need. Try creating a time to work on feeling a sense of home within yourself.

What do you need internally to feel safe and secure? No matter what's happening externally?

I've found great value in the ability to feel at home within myself, especially when there are extreme circumstances happening around me.

Suppose I'm walking in a park, and, suddenly, somebody starts arguing with another. Yes, I'm aware that arguing is happening. I feel safe and secure within myself, and, depending, on the situation, it might be wise to find a different path to walk. It doesn't change my sense of home and internal safety.

Let's say you've gone on a vacation and have this expectation about how it will be. When you arrive, it's nothing like what you expected. You could feel incredibly disappointed, which will create a bad mood. If there's truly nothing you can do about it, then why focus on the negative at that point? Being at home within yourself means it doesn't matter if the air conditioning works, the view is what you had hoped, or the bed is as soft as you had imagined. A sense of home within creates a sense of calmness and acceptance.

As you make time for this practice, maybe use a notebook or computer. I like to speak my notes, so I usually have my phone near me to document what I'm feeling, what I'm experiencing, and how I would like it to be different. That way, I can see the full picture. Then I can start working on the opposite quality needed to balance, regardless of the external circumstances. So, in the example of the vacation, If the place I've rented isn't what I had hoped, being upset about it will throw me out of balance; accepting it would be better and even feeling grateful would be optimum. I first have to reconcile my feelings to come to a place of acceptance.

Realize that your world is only a reflection of yourself and stop finding fault with the reflection. Attend to yourself first, set yourself right, mentally and emotionally. The physical self will follow automatically.

-Nisargadatta Maharaj

 Work on creating the inner home, and, eventually, the outer will reflect your efforts.

 The possibilities are endless.

 Your home the way YOU want it.

Chapter 11

Moving through Fight, Flight, or Freeze

Let's talk about movement and how to move these experiences that are stuck within you, the impressions that need to be lifted from the body-mind system. If you've ever been in a fight, whether physical, verbal, or energetic, you know this energy. You may be looking for a battle because all that energy is trying to move, intensely looking for resistance from an opposing force. That same energy that's trying to move is also responsible for the fleeing. I'm sure you can remember a moment when every part of you wanted to get away from or out of a situation. Depending on the dominating quality behind this energy, you'll either fight, flee, or freeze. What if we could learn to move with this energy and intensity with more awareness? I absolutely don't like the feeling of being taken over by such power and then acting from that place with a lack of understanding. I feel controlled by the experience, and I'm looking to have more awareness to change that experience.

Movement with sound or music is beneficial during this process. Try finding some instrumental music to move with so you start feeling your own body and flow. I don't recommend music with lyrics, as you may find yourself lost in the story of those words, and you're trying to create more awareness of what's moving through you. When I first started consciously moving/dancing, I noticed how awkward I felt, so I stayed with the awkwardness (Explore phase 1). What was behind that was self-judgment. Here I was, alone in my house, awkwardly moving and judging every part of it. This was great! I needed to work on my self-judgment around movement, and as I looked at it directly, a memory came (Discover Phase 2). I was six years old, wearing a beautiful yellow dress with matching undershorts dancing freely in the front room. I had no self-judgment, and then my mother entered the room with a raised voice and judgmental tone asking, "What do you think you're doing?" I stopped, confused. She then continued, "You're trying to seduce your father! From now on, there will be no more dresses or dancing. Do you understand me ?!" A moment of pure childhood bliss shut down and judged with a big word that made no sense to a six-year-old and then a reprimand that implied that what I was experiencing was wrong.

The movement practice brought up a core moment that pointed out when I was told what to believe and think, and that wasn't in alignment with who I was. It was one of many moments when self-doubt had been ingrained and impressed upon me. I continued to move and dance through this belief and judgment until I felt free as a bird. I had many sessions working through this one, so have patience and don't give up on yourself.

How can you use movement and awareness when you're aware that fight, flight, or freeze is happening?

You need the opposite quality to change a habit that has also become ingrained. The fight, flight, or freeze response is incredibly powerful. Your heart rate and blood pressure increase, your blood flow is being redirected, you may have pale or flushed skin, pupils will dilate to bring in more light, and the sensation of pain may be reduced until you feel safe again. The senses become heightened as you see and hear things you may not usually notice, creating a feeling of being on edge. Your memory can be affected from clear and vivid to a complete blackout of the incident; You may be tense or trembling, since stress hormones circulate throughout your body. Your bodily functions may be affected, which aligns with the phrase, "He scared the crap out of me." All jokes aside, this experience is quite visceral, and we're designed to have this response as a way to protect ourselves from grave danger.

With trauma, we perceive a threat when there's most likely no danger; this is why we need to go back and question those triggers to reduce the power of the belief that there's life-threatening danger when there is none. I've had experiences with all three responses, and they're miserable and exhausting during and after. My triggers would mostly begin with fight and end up with fleeing and running away or with freeze variations. I remember a trigger I had early in my relationship with my current husband. I reacted to something he said with a fighting response and then immediately walked out, got in my car, and drove to the beach an hour away, ranting and raving during my drive. By the time I made it to the beach, I couldn't remember why I was upset and was even more shocked to see him pull up behind me. My first thought was that he was crazy and stalking me. The reality was that he was concerned by my response and was following me to make sure I was safe, since I was driving triggered. Poor guy, I was used to this type of reaction, but he wasn't. His trigger responses were very different than mine. As you can see, a trigger response can create unintentional trauma for others when it hasn't healed.

The body naturally will move during a fight or flight response, so the idea here is to become more aware of that movement and consciously direct it, instead of being taken over by it.

If you have healthy people in your life who support your healing, you can always tell them the new things you might try during your triggers to come out of them quicker. If not, no worries; you're working toward becoming your own best friend.

I like to notice my hands as the fight response can show up as a physical fight. I start by opening and closing my hands to bring more awareness vs. the closed fist that may happen when preparing for a fight. If you've been living with your triggers for some time, I'm sure you're already aware of the thoughts and behaviors during this time. The more awareness you create, the less charge the trigger will have over you.

I then start rolling my shoulders, the visual of a boxer preparing for his fight comes up. To clarify, you're not preparing for a fight; you're preparing for presence and the ability to resist the fight response. I move my head, stretching both sides of my neck, and take a big deep breath. My thoughts, at this point, could vary from *Stay calm; you're safe to Jeannine, the feeling of fighting is an unconscious and old response; remember courage and commitment to overcome this habit.* I recognize that you may not be in that place yet and that your thoughts may be different. In trying to remember the earlier days of triggers, there was so much profanity that I was silently sending toward my perceived attacker that it was challenging for rational thoughts to be heard if there were any rational thoughts.

You can only begin from where you are, so be with it and do your best not to act on the feeling or thought. Stay with the awareness of consciously moving different body parts to stay aware. If you know that you're a great verbal fighter, try to move the thoughts of what clever response you'll say with your breath. Sometimes it can be helpful to imagine that the intensity of what you are feeling is going somewhere. You could imagine the ocean receiving this intensity on the inbreath and cooling it down on the outbreath so that you are not spewing fire or venom; this feels like you're trying to tame a dragon, which is a great accomplishment, so don't give up. Even if you stay in this place with your trigger for some time, it's an improvement from where you have been. Celebrate all the victories, no matter what the perceived size of them are. I would often say to myself during these triggers, "Try something different, Jeannine; your life isn't in danger, and the body-mind is having a past response to a present moment. What am I not seeing that indicates my life is truly not in danger?" This last question was a way to question the circumstance of perceived threat, which is amazingly powerful if you can remember to use it. The power to question everything is what I call a superpower because it transforms the perception of trauma that has been on repeat and replay since the actual time of trauma. There will come a time when the energy of a physical or verbal fight is so strong that something has to be done to expel this energy. I often would use working out. I even found kickboxing useful; however, there's a fine line between expelling the energy and stirring it back up, even increasing it. Eventually, I discovered that kickboxing was increasing the fight; like increases like.

I found that using video journaling helpful as this allowed me to go back and watch these videos, observing myself in my triggered state. I would rant all through the video, then eventually break down and cry from this misery. You can always go back and delete the video, but I would encourage you to keep it long enough to go back and observe yourself until you're no longer triggered by watching it or judgmental of yourself. When I would rewatch my videos, I slowly began to see the part of me stuck in the trauma time loop, begging for help to get out. I genuinely wanted to help this part of me, and, since I was committed to the relationship with myself, I kept working on this.

Similarly, an addict can only recover once they realize they have a problem and want to change; only you can decide if you want this to change. Once the commitment is there, then have courage to keep working on it with persistence and consistency. You got this! I have faith in you! Do you have faith in yourself?!

Fight response

This is characterized by a quick verbal response, interrupting or speaking over someone during an interaction, thinking about what you'll say next or how the action will hurt the other (an energetic punch), and a desire to fight, push, hit physically, etc.

Now you have the opportunity to change the habit of fighting.

Step 1: Breathe. Wherever the breath goes, the mind follows.

Try moving your body. I sometimes rock back and forth from side to side or maybe move in a square dance shape. The idea here's to make movement more conscious, so you're less likely to move unconsciously. I use the imagery of a lion about to pounce. Do I want to be the lion that pounces before it realizes its surroundings (that wouldn't be a smart lion), or do I want to be the lion moving with intelligence? If you've ever watched a lion in the wild, they move with intention only once they have observed their prey and the surrounding threats, and then they wait. I'm not preparing you to pounce; I'm showing you your animal instinct. There's a time and place where pouncing may be needed, for example, if a mugger were trying to steal from you. I'm showing you how to tame your animal. It would be better to know that you can unleash and pounce on your prey and consciously choose not to, than to be driven by the unconscious force of that energy and end up doing something you probably will regret.

Connecting with your breath allows you to tame that ferocious lion or lioness.

When I'm in a fight-triggered response, my husband calls this aspect of me Ferocia for her ferocious, lioness like qualities. Now, that alone would trigger me in the early days. I now see it as his way of pointing out that I'm fighting. I take a deep breath. The first one is entirely charged. My inner dialogue is often fighting back while another part of me is remembering that Ferocia is my fight-triggered aspect, and this is just a cue from my accountability partner that I'm in a triggered state. I'll either continue breathing or laugh as I acknowledge where I am, allowing for change. Being able to laugh at yourself takes some time and is a great relief once you get there.

Step 2: Acknowledge that you're in a fighting triggered space.

The power of seeing something as it is is profound.

Step3: Ask for a pause or time out.

There's no need to explain why you need it. I find that holding up two fingers or the time out sign is an effective way to make this happen. Followed by, "Hold that thought; I need a moment to gather myself. This conversation is vital to me, and I'm not in the space to be able to have that conversation now." Eight times out of ten, this works, unless, of course, the other party is also triggered, in which case a more direct statement may be needed. For example, "It seems we aren't communicating at our optimum, and I'll need to reschedule this conversation." Make sure you do reschedule it so that you're not avoiding it. It's quite mature to acknowledge that the present moment may not be right to continue, but it's relatively immature to avoid it altogether. Let's face it; if that relationship interaction comes to a resolution sooner rather than later, whether it's a resolution of growth or separation, it's highly recommended to deal with things as they come. Otherwise, you may find yourself brooding, which is no different than what was happening earlier, except you have now moved the fight to an energetic plane vs. the physical and verbal plane as before. Nothing will have changed by avoiding.

Step 4: Explore yourself. Meaning look at what your current state is. When did it shift? Was it something that was said? Was it a look? Maybe their body language? Was it a smell? Was it a thought you had?

Keep moving if you're still feeling the fight; this is a great practice to move and ask yourself these questions.

Step 5: Discover all the above aspects to see what happened inside of you.

Remember, the other person involved only triggered that which was already inside of you. If you're pointing the finger, then look at the other three pointing back at you.

Notice in the image how tightly gripped the thumb is around the three fingers. This image depicts perfectly a triggered person, placing blame with finger-pointing and no awareness of the three being pointed back. The thumb shows the mighty strength behind avoiding looking at it.

What are the three fingers pointing out?

1. This trigger is your teacher
2. Question your thoughts, beliefs, and actions at this moment.
3. Face Everything And Rise (F.E.A.R)

Being willing to face yourself and rise above the fight is where the real power is. Pointing the finger and not looking at yourself is a fear response.

Step 6: Heal. Healing can now begin. Take all that you've discovered and start giving that part of you that's triggered the wisdom, compassion, and love needed to become whole. I'll refer to how to do this in my example below with the 3-year-old version of myself when we get to the freeze section.

Step 7: Integrate. Once healing has happened, you can now integrate-join with the disconnected part of you to become more whole. The triggered version of you is disconnected and stuck in a time loop of memory from the past. Once you heal that aspect, you naturally integrate.

Step 8: Relate. You're now an upgraded version of yourself, having integrated with the disconnected aspect. You have to get to know yourself with this integration. I call this the dating yourself time. I mean, isn't that what you do when you begin a relationship? You date to get to know the person; the same thing applies here.

Flight response

This is characterized by an uncontrollable urge to run away from a situation, avoid something or someone. I know this one oh so well. The first thing I recommend is to take a few deep breaths and notice how the body wants to move away. Then try moving from side to side, putting all your weight on one leg and then the next. This way, your body is moving with that energy. If you're able, ask yourself, why you want to run away. What's the perceived threat? The idea is to create more presence in these experiences. After all, the Fight, Flight, or Freeze response is all about past trauma disguised by the belief that the trauma is happening again. It lacks presence. The more presence practice you have during these moments, the better. Changing from a pattern begins with the first step toward doing something different.

Freeze response

The freeze response is fascinating because you literally feel as if you're frozen or stuck and can't move.

1. Try to connect with your breath. The deeper the breaths, the more movement is happening internally to support you in coming out of the freeze.
2. Then move your eyes around, left to right, right to left, up and down, circle toward the right and then the left.
3. Identify three things in the space you're in to bring presence to this moment. I prefer to find three living things to represent life and nature, since we're connected to nature, and there's consciousness within nature that supports being present.
4. Next is limbs' movement, maybe swing your arms, move your legs, wiggle your toes and fingers. Any movement is helpful to unfreeze.
5. Once you can move, you could try an inner dialogue to start Exploring what made you freeze. Was it a sound, smell, something you saw, someone, etc.?
6. Once you've Discovered what made you freeze from the questioning in step 5, you can move onto the Healing of that version of you that had a past response to a current situation. Usually, it's

the version of you that experienced that particular trauma.

Often, a loud noise would trigger the freeze response in me. As I Explored my memory of loud noises, I Discovered a moment early on in my childhood when a frightened 3-year-old version of me was in shock by the loud yelling that seemed to come out of nowhere between my parents. When I observed her, she was frightened by the loud noises and at what she was seeing. She was watching her parents physically fighting. I could see that she needed love, support, reassurance, and to be unfrozen from this memory. I came to her, held her hand, looked into her eyes, and asked, "Would you like to go to a quieter and safer place?" She agreed, and we went to a place in nature with butterflies and a beautiful river, which created a feeling of calm for her. I explained to her that her parents were sick, and that's why they behaved that way. I reassured her that I would be caring for her now so that she didn't have to experience these scary moments.

Essentially, what I'm doing here, is giving the 3-year-old version of me a different experience to unfreeze her from that moment. This was a disconnected version of myself that had been stuck at this moment since it happened. That's why the adult version of me would freeze, and the repressed memory of trauma would replay and repeat. By identifying this disconnected version of myself and giving her a different experience to unfreeze her from this trauma time loop, Healing begins and then Integration with this part of myself. The new venture was a healthy adult (present me) embodying mother's wisdom, giving the 3-year-old the nourishing mother's love, support, and trust, created a different scenario where she was no longer stuck watching her parents fight. The water movement in the lake, along with the butterfly and my loving words and touch, created a healthier experience.

I then committed to her that I would never leave her; this is important since there was a disconnect to begin with, so a commitment of trust is necessary for healing and integration. I'm taking full responsibility for this version of myself. She's no longer at the mercy of her parents. Once the commitment has been accepted, integration naturally begins. That hole that was created by the disconnect from trauma is now becoming whole. Now comes the fun part. Who are you now that you're more whole? You get to know yourself as an upgraded version. I found that I was much more playful, and my ability to be creative was no longer stuck or stagnant. My daughters noticed a difference, as well as my husband. There was a lightness to my being; I was more playful and curious with all the qualities that a 3-year-old has. This integration is extraordinary now that I'm a grandmother. The ability to play and be curious with my grandkids is the best part of being a grandma. I am now Relating differently with myself and others.

Flight, Fight, Freeze, Freedom.

 Wherever the breath goes the mind follows.

 Stop and just breathe, move your eyes, arms, and legs.

 Don't make any decisions until you're free.

 What are the three fingers pointing out?
1.This trigger is your teacher.
2.Question your thoughts, beliefs, and actions at this moment.
3.Face Everything And Rise (F.E.A.R.)

Chapter 12

Identifying Your Allies, Anger, and Dialogue

Identify who your well-wishing allies are in your life. These are people you trust in your worst moments who are aligned with your growth to come out of triggered states.

Ask these well-wishers ahead of time, when you're not triggered, if they would be willing to support you if they notice you're triggered by doing the following:

1. Show you that you're in a safe environment.
2. Remind you that they aren't your enemy.
3. Remind you about and join you in deep breathing.
4. Guide you in a locational practice, identifying the nature around you, plants, sunlight, flowers, or any object representing the present.

5. Lovingly touch or embrace you with words that represent the present.
6. Encourage you to use "I feel" statements
7. Provide a safe space for movement and possibly for you to make loud noises should you need to move through sound.

If you're so triggered that you can't trust even your well-wishers, then remember this one crucial piece of wisdom.

DON'T MAKE ANY DECISIONS FROM A TRIGGERED STATE

Give yourself a timeout until the brain comes back online for executive decision making. The caution here is that you don't regret the decisions you made, including steering your life in a direction you hadn't intended.

ANGER is a messenger

Don't shoot the messenger! Anger is a signal arising deep from within that needs to be seen and heard so you can begin healing. It's easy to let anger run the show or even try to ignore it, but its power comes bubbling up like a volcano, eventually begging to be witnessed.

How do we honor and respect anger?

A part of you is trying to get your attention. Stop ignoring yourself. Honor and respect every aspect. You're incredible, and there's an intelligence that's trying to get your attention. Once you realize that anger is a messenger, you're more likely to be willing to take the journey of talking with your anger.

Create a safe space to explore this fierce emotion, a space where you can stomp your feet, scream (screaming into a pillow works), and write, or maybe you're brave enough to video your process to reflect on later. You'll need water to stay hydrated and tissue for crying. You may also want to include an old phone book that can be ripped and destroy, giving anger an outlet. I suggest working with a practitioner if you feel that trying this out on your own is too intense. As you get familiar with anger, you'll become comfortable with it as it comes.

If you live with others, let them know you're about to explore some intense emotions or go into a healing session, and there may be loud sounds. They don't need to worry; however, give them and idea of when they should come to check on you, especially if this is something new that you're exploring.

Now that you're ready, let's explore the Who, What, When, Where, and Why of your anger.

Who triggered the anger reaction?

What does anger want to say? Record it or write it down as you express it. Did some words or interactions allow anger to present itself?

When is a time you felt the same way? Try to get to the most intense and earliest memory.

Where do you feel anger? Scan your body from head to toe if you're unsure.

Why is anger here?

Have you ignored a part of yourself?

Are there boundaries that need to be learned?

Are you doing what you've been told you should do instead of checking to see if that's true for you?

In my experience, I was so judgmental and embarrassed by my anger. I felt like there must be something wrong with me to have such intense feelings. When I started exploring and conversing with anger, I discovered many aspects of different ages. The adolescent version of me had the most charge behind it, having been told that my feelings weren't true. My accomplishments weren't my own. They were a result of being my mother's daughter.

I needed to befriend this aspect and first allow her to throw a fit.

I yelled out, "My accomplishments are a result of my hard work despite you!"

"My feelings are valid and not for you to decide whether they're right or wrong!"

I continued to yell out as if my mother were there until I had nothing left to say. I finally heard the anger that had built up. After I was finished, I could see that what was behind my anger was sadness and fear of not being heard and acknowledged. Often, the feeling of sadness or fear is hiding behind anger. Anger is the messenger trying to point out the deeper sadness or fear. Sadness needs the flow of tears to open the heart, and fear needs to be seen. When either of these are ignored, then anger shows up with a message to be heard.

It doesn't matter if the person you're angry with hears it; it's more important that you're aware of it, you see and listen to it. I committed to myself that I would acknowledge my accomplishments and feelings. I created healthier boundaries in relationships and began communicating clearly for my sake and others.

Positive to counteract Negative

There will be plenty of opportunities to practice the power of positive thinking. You first need to be able to recognize your negative thought patterns to begin this practice. For example, what's your first thought upon waking? Is it positive and optimistic or negative and pessimistic?

The most uncomplicated thoughts to identify are the ones when we aren't in a triggered state. I recommend starting there, and, over time, you'll be able to notice your thought patterns during and after a trigger.

When I began observing them, I noticed that my thoughts leaned more toward negative and pessimistic around specific subjects like close relationships. My thought was that the person would betray me somehow, which prevented me from opening up in any relationship. I decided to work on reframing that thought with a positive. The new thought was that I was open to the possibility of a close relationship where trust happens. I didn't replace the thought with *This person will not betray me*, as that was unrealistic per my personal experiences and uses the negating word "Not."

It's important to honor that your previous life experiences have gotten you to where you are today. To change the negative patterns and impressions from those experiences, we need to counteract them with the opposite quality.

Negative words:

https://www.enchantedlearning.com/wordlist/negativewords.shtml

Positive words:

https://www.enchantedlearning.com/wordlist/positivewords.shtml

Who are your well-wishers?

Anger is the messenger trying to point out the deeper sadness or fear.

Sadness needs the flow of tears to open the heart, and fear needs to be seen. When either of these are ignored, then anger shows up with a message to be heard.

What's the message from Anger?

What words are you using and thinking?

Change your words and thinking to positive to counteract the negative speaking and thinking.

Chapter 13

Client Cases

"Every disturbing and depressing thought that enters the Manas (mind) has a simultaneous effect on every cell of the body and tends to produce diseases."[1]

Physical Pain Case

Elizabeth came in with chronic right shoulder pain and had been to doctors and physical therapists, but no one could find anything wrong. She complained of an ache that wouldn't go away. It was a perfect example of the body giving a clear trigger response to an impression. She was looking for relief and expecting bodywork, so I said, "What if we try something different, and if you still have the pain after, I'll give you a free bodywork session?" She was skeptical and curious. "The doctors, physical thera-

---

1   Kayachikitsa Volume 3, Manasa Roga Prakarna: Visesa pg. 475 By: Dr.P.S. Byadgi and Dr. A.K. Pandey

pists, MRI, CT scans, and blood work say there's nothing wrong, so what do you have to lose by trying something completely different?" I asked. Of course, I was referring to using the EDHIR® process. She agreed to try.

As she connected with her breath and dropped into her body, I had her focus on her right shoulder and explored this area by describing what she felt. She described a deep ache. Does this feeling remind you of something or someone? I asked. Her lips quivered, so I knew we were getting close to the source of her pain. The pain reminded her of her dad. Her dad passed a year ago. I encouraged her to keep exploring this ache that triggered the memory of her dad. She took a few deep breaths, and the tears came pouring out. We were now reaching the Discovery phase. As she cried, I asked her what was happening, and she expressed that she just wanted her dad to be proud of her and wanted to tell him how much she loved him. She felt sorry for not being successful. Now moving into the Healing phase, I asked her if she thought she could approach this version of her dad she was seeing. She nodded, yes.

It seemed to me that what she needed was to tell her father how she felt and for him to be proud of her. However, I've learned never to assume, as this can limit one's healing. As she approached her father, she stated that his back was facing her, and he wouldn't turn around and face her as she wanted. I asked her how old she seems to be at this moment with her dad. There was a long pause and her lip quivered again. She whimpered as she answered, "16 years old." I asked if something happen at 16 that's familiar to the scene she was experiencing. She responded that she was mixed up with the wrong crowd and failed some of her classes. Dad had been cold, distant, and seemingly very disappointed in her from that point on. A conversation needed to happen between Dad and daughter regarding this moment. I guided her in calling out to her Dad to get his attention. As she did this, he turned around and looked past her as if she weren't even there. I said, "Look around the room; is there something that stands out as odd or unique?" She said there was a gold whistle. "Try blowing the whistle to see if that gets Dad's attention." It worked! She explained that it was as if it snapped him out of a state he was in, yet his eyes were so sorrowful.

"What would you like to ask or say to your dad?" I guided her to speak directly to him for this healing to begin. She began crying again, and she expressed her deep sorrow for disappointing him and wished that the relationship hadn't changed after 16 years old. He looked confused and then responded. "My darling girl, I'm the one who should be apologizing. I was too wrapped up in my work to see that you needed more support, and I let you down. I've never forgiven myself for that." She was shocked by this response. Her perception and interpretation of that time were not at all what she believed. It was true that she felt rejected by her dad but not because he was rejecting her. It was because he couldn't face her due to his disappointment in himself. At this point, I guided her to ask or tell him anything and everything she wanted (especially since he had passed). Elizabeth poured her heart out for the next 10 minutes until she felt she had said everything she wanted to say. Dad and daughter embraced, and she watched him walk away. I had Elizabeth stay with this feeling as she entered into the Integration phase. From her perception of this experience, the disconnected part had created such disappointment that she became stuck in a time loop. Her right shoulder was carrying this pain around, trying to get her attention. As she healed this, the disconnection began connecting, integrating.

I slowly guided her back to the present time and space. As she opened her eyes and identified three living things in my office, the plant, water fountain, and flowers, she was back in the present time and space. She started rotating her right shoulder, looking for the deep ache. It wasn't there. Now the Relating phase had begun. In the coming weeks, she reported many changes. Her depression episodes, which she hadn't mentioned before, had subsided. She found that her relationship with her husband had unusually improved, and she noticed she was communicating differently and more confidently. The shoulder pain didn't return.

A case of Disgust:

Amber came in one day and was ranting about her husband and his lack of support and help with their newborn child. She also noticed she just felt disgusted by him when he came home, and she felt so angry all the time. I happened to know already that she was abused as a child, so I knew there was some healing to do here; however, she had no memory of this abuse and wasn't ready to go to that space in the past. I asked her many what if questions, trying to explore her more profound pain.

I want to point out that, in my experience, it's not necessary to relive past experiences. However, it is essential to find the aspects of yourself that have been disconnected because that disconnect is creating pain, discomfort, and stagnation in your life, among other things.

Amber's mind was extraordinary at being able to deflect and avoid answering, so I knew I was on the right track and getting closer to the source.

I was trying to get her to a place where she could feel her pain and discomfort. The questioning was a way of getting there.

I decided to go for it and asked her directly, "What if there's a little girl version of you, a little Amber, who has an impression that's before you could remember, that's related to the idea of the father? What if that's true? What if your feelings toward your husband, whom you see as a father now, trigger this response in you?"

The tears squirted from Amber's eyes, and her pain came pouring out. Can you see this little Amber? I asked. She could see her in a way she had never experienced before. I asked her to approach this little one and ask her what she needs.

"She wants to play with her father without the play turning into something else." As Amber cried and expressed how she couldn't understand how a father could do such things to his child, I said, "People who don't heal from their pain end up creating harm, even if they had no intention of doing so. It doesn't excuse the behavior, of course."

Her inner child, little Amber, expressed that she wanted to go and be with her mom and a dad who would play with her appropriately. I guided her to take the child by her hand and walk her to her mom and the appropriate father. She began to smirk and chuckle and said, "Of course, my adoptive dad is here."

(She had always had a love/hate relationship with him, and I suspect it was due to this particular wound of the first father impression). She cried more as she realized when watching her adoptive dad play with the grandkids, which included her daughter, that that was what she needed in her younger years. She let the little version of herself play as a child should, without fear, with her mom and adoptive dad.

After some time, I asked her to make a promise to little Amber. She made a promise to this version of her inner child that she would never leave her or ignore her again. (Amber was ignoring her when the pain would come, and she would push it away.) As the little one played, I guided Amber back using the relationship with her breath and body to secure the connection with her bigger self. As she opened her eyes and identified three objects around her that represented the present time and space, Amber realized her feelings and how she perceived her husband weren't entirely true anymore. Amber said, "Boy, do I have some apologizing to do!"

In this case, her pain, which she was ignoring, essentially missing a part of herself, had become a projection onto her husband, as seeing him in the father role brought up all of her unresolved father wounds. The triggering factor was the feeling that her husband wasn't doing what he should have been. On its own, it wasn't a clear indicator; it was combined with how she felt in other areas of the relationship. Since Amber was disconnected from an aspect of herself, her relationship with herself wasn't complete, which meant her other relationships, like her marriage, would end up pointing out this imbalance. Why is that? Healthy relationships begin with the one that you have with yourself. The unhealthy aspects within yourself will naturally show up in other relationships because that naturally happens when you start relating. Relationships point out where we can grow. As we connect with others, if we're staying true to ourselves, we'll notice areas that need work

Case of Chronic Indigestion, fatty liver, and anger

Kai presented with chronic indigestion after having his gallbladder removed over a year ago.

We worked on diet and used some Ayurvedic formulations, which began helping immediately. What I found fascinating in this case is that I always had a feeling that he had more to share with me about his life but wasn't comfortable or trusting yet. By the third follow-up, his indigestion had reduced and he was actively working on breathing through the anger. Up to this point, the anger was being triggered by coworkers, yet I knew this was the surface. During this visit, he opened up about his 20-year love affair with his best friend and how he had been waiting for him to finally leave his wife so that they could be together. He had seen multiple therapists to help with ending this relationship, yet still he could not. He knew that his best friend was never going to leave his wife. "Do you think you could help me with that?" he asked. I said,

"How about instead of focusing on ending something, we focus on the relationship you have with yourself in every aspect, and if change is going to happen, it naturally will?"

He liked this idea, so we began the journey of Kai dating himself essentially. This case went so deep into his 20-year marriage to his wife and discovering he was gay and too afraid to come out. It stayed a secret through this love affair with his friend. My instincts led me to a place where we used the EDHIR® process and discovered that he wasn't able to see himself; his experiences were through others and his validation of himself was through the actions and behaviors of his lover and best friend. As Kai started getting to know himself better, without the identity of his lover, he began sleeping better, learned better boundaries during moments that always pulled him back into places he felt were unhealthy. His choices naturally changed as he changed. At times, he would ask if he should break up with his lover, and I said, "You'll know if that's what you need to do when the time comes, and it'll be so clear to you that you won't need anyone to validate that decision. My intention was to guide him toward being his own lover, best friend, and, eventually, his own father. The better he knew himself the better decisions would line up to support his growth. I had no attachment or judgment of the outcome of this story. If Kai and his lover were going to be together or if Kai, on his own, discovered he wanted something different that wasn't a secret.

Kai's relationship with himself is the key ingredient for stability in other relationships. This included his indigestion, fatty liver, and anger. Once the relationship with digestion in gut, mind, and heart was in balance, the rest would fall into place.

Over the next year, Kai blossomed in all aspects of life. The source of the anger came from not being acknowledged or seen by his father growing up. He was craving that which led to the relationship with his best friend in which he felt seen on one side and a secret on the other. Kai naturally spent less time with his friend, as who he was becoming was no longer in alignment with that relationship. The clarity of this decision was so empowering for him. He learned to take care of himself on all levels. The anger was seen, and behind it was sadness. Once sadness was flowing, the heart released and so did the mind, creating space for something new. Kai has begun exploring new relationships that aren't a secret, his indigestion went away, and the liver levels came down to normal. The anger was his messenger, and each time it was triggered by coworkers, it was in situations where he didn't feel seen. When there's a block in the system, an accumulation happens on one end and a depletion on the other. Once the flow was restored, balance naturally happened.

 The relationship between our physical, mental, emotional & digestive systems determines our overall health & wellness.

 The answers we are looking for are inside; we must be willing to see and hear them for change.

Chapter 14

5 Key Ingredients for Health and Healing Using the Ancient Wisdom of Ayurveda.

It's of great importance that I speak about how Ayurveda helped me in my journey of healing in body and mind and helped many of my clients in their healing journey. The profound impact it has had in my life prompted me to study this science and art form in great depth.

I first need to acknowledge my Vaidya (Ayurvedic Doctor), Dr. Jayarajan Kodikannath. I came in for my first consult after having an episode of passing out after intense pressure in the top of my head. This included what seemed like a seizure accompanied by an out-of-body experience where I could see myself lying on the floor and my husband trying to help me. When I came back into my body, I couldn't see, and my hands and feet felt like ice. It took a good 30 minutes before my sight came back, and even though I should have gone to the emergency room, I just knew that I needed to lie still and not be around many people. The next day, I went in and got checked out by an M.D. There were no signs of seizure or stroke. I began to describe the out-of-body experience and quickly assessed that this wasn't the place to share such information, as I may have been sent to the psych ward, so I withheld that information. They ran blood tests, MRIs, and brain wave activity. There seemed to be an adhesion on my left thalamus. They concluded that they couldn't confirm if it had been there before this incident. My brain wave activity was very slow and the technician stated that she usually saw this in elderly patients.

The official diagnosis was that I had a "spell." I double checked that I was hearing them clearly, and they stated for a second time that, in fact, I had a spell. So, my first thought was, *I must need a witch doctor since I had a spell.* I'm only partly joking here. There were no medicines to offer or treatment plan except that they wanted to test the brain activity in 3 months. I went to sleep that evening and had the most peculiar dream in which I was in India—I had never been there—and I entered a cave where a yogi with a long beard told me that the only way to heal was through Ayurveda. I woke the next morning and shared my dream with my husband, who encouraged me to follow that trail. I looked up the nearest Doctor of Ayurveda which happened to be 10 minutes from the home we had just moved into. I found this to be very serendipitous and called to make the appointment with Dr. Jay. My only understanding of Ayurveda before this dream was a lovely book gifted to me by my husband back in 2012 by Dr. David Frawley called *Yoga & Ayurveda*. I enjoyed it so much that I went on to read *Ayurveda and the Mind*, which was the book I was in the middle of reading when I passed out.

Dr. Jay spent 90 minutes with me asking every type of question imaginable about every aspect of my life. Afterwards, he calmly and compassionately told me he had a plan and understood what was happening with me. I was in awe. He asked more questions than any doctor I had ever seen. He checked my nails, eyes, tongue, skin, and pulse, which seemed odd to me at the time. The Ayurvedic assessment was that Vata (air and space) along with Pitta (fire and water), were extremely out of balance. The symptoms showed up in the mind, nervous system, gastrointestinal system, respiratory system, menstrual system, muscular system, and urinary system. This was a result of the imbalances and extremes that my body and mind had gone through thus far.

Ayurveda is the science of life that originated in India over 5,000 years ago. We are directly connected with the rhythm of nature and the five elements, and when the natural rhythm becomes disrupted the elements become imbalanced and disease happens. Creating a balanced and harmonious rhythm creates a strong foundation for health.

We use three words to describe all five elements.

- Vata, the principle of movement and dynamism, is a combination of space and air.
- Pitta, the energy of transformation, is a combination of fire and water.

- Kapha, the energy of cohesion, is a combination of earth and water.

The path of health and wellness is determined by your lifestyle and routine (Vihara) and your inputs (Ahara).

The five key ingredients for stability using the ancient wisdom of Ayurveda are:

1. Lifestyle and routine.
2. Perception
3. Breath
4. Food
5. Water

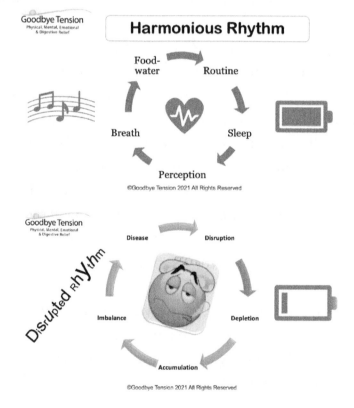

Lifestyle and Routine

Your lifestyle and routine rhythm are set based on your sleep cycle. When you sleep determines when you wake, when you eat, your ability to use all your faculties, and your ability to take care of yourself.

Sleep is the mind at rest. At certain times of day, the elements are at their strongest; Pitta, the energy of transformation and digestion is from 10 pm to 2 am and from 10 am to 2 pm.

Mental digestion happens when the mind is at rest during sleep from 10 pm to 2 am. This is very important for everyone to maintain a healthy rhythm and balance. For those of us who've had trauma and adverse life experiences, it's critical to have a consistent sleep pattern that begins at or before 10 pm so that all of the undigested mental and emotional impressions and experiences can start digesting.

Good sleep hygiene includes:

- Turning off all digital devices an hour or more before bed
- Calming breath practice such as deep diaphragmatic or alternate nostril breathing
- Dimmed lights an hour before bed
- Relaxing music

Some herbs and formulations help this mental digestion process. I'm only referencing them here, and I don't recommend you take them without the proper guidance. They are Guduchi, Kalyanaka Ghritam, Manasamitra Vatakam, Ashwagandha, Shankapushpi, Brahmi, and Brahmi Ghritam.

If you choose to take these herbs and formulations without the proper guidance from an experienced Ayurvedic Practitioner or Vaidya (Ayurvedic Doctor), you can create more imbalance in your system.

What happens when you miss the mental digestion hours of 10 pm to 2 am?

You may get a burst of energy allowing for more tasks to be done, staying up into the wee hours of the morning. Many people refer to themselves as "Night Owls" for this reason. This burst of energy comes at a cost eventually. Our body rejuvenates and repairs during sleep, sleep is mind at rest and mind needs to digest. Many long-term imbalances come from improper sleep habits. Some of these imbalances include:

- Memory issues
- Trouble with thinking and concentrating
- Accidents
- Mood changes
- Weakened Immunity
- Weight gain
- High blood pressure
- Risk for Diabetes
- Risk for Heart Disease
- Low sex drive

I can tell you from personal experience that when I first came to Ayurveda, I wasn't sleeping until 3 am and waking up sometime around 9:30 am to begin my day. I learned that any eight hours of sleep isn't the same as the proper 8 hours of sleep. Again, the timing is the most important. Moving back my sleep cycle from 3 am to 10 pm would have been a shock to my system if I tried to make a massive shift all at once. For anyone who's struggling with any dis-ease, trauma, imbalance, etc., slow and steady is how they want to make these changes, making small incremental changes, trying to slowly adjust their clock so that there's no sudden shock to the system. What I usually recommend for my clients to do and what I learned to do for myself was to start moving back the sleep time by 30-minute intervals. I was sleeping around 3 am and would try to go to sleep at 2:30 am, for about two weeks, until it became a habit, and then I would move back again. I was able to make adjustments by the hour, and that seemed to work, probably because my mind and body were craving that mental digestion that was now happening, since I was beginning to sleep at the correct time.

I knew that I could make those changes in a way that worked best for me, my family dynamic, and my schedule. The concept and fundamental principle is to avoid making extreme changes. The body doesn't like extremes, and the mind certainly doesn't like extremes. Trauma, in which the fight, flight, or freeze mechanism has activated, is an extreme experience, becoming a strain to your mind-body system. You must nurture the mind and body to slowly come into balance, not create more trauma by trying to force balance. I must tell you this because certain personality types, after I advise them to make this drastic change, can quickly and easily do it. Some cannot. It's important to know what your personality is and the healthiest way to approach it. In my healing journey, I treated my healing as if I were running a marathon that never ended. That's part of what brought me to the science of Ayurveda. I had utterly depleted myself from the weight loss journey and the intensity of approaching my healing.

Once the sleep schedule is aligned, naturally, the food and the eating patterns will fall into place. Through the Ayurvedic lens, a new cycle begins with one Muhurta, which is 48 minutes. This means when your schedule for eating and sleeping shifts beyond that 48-minute window, your body and mind adjust to another cycle. For example, if I go to bed at 10 pm Monday through Friday and on Saturday I go to bed at 11 pm, My harmonious cycle that was becoming stable through the week's consistency is now beginning a new cycle. If this inconsistency becomes a pattern, I will have less stability than if I maintain the consistent cycle of sleep at 10 pm.

Of course, you have to consider life and what's happening; it's not always possible, but if you have that wisdom and understanding, you're more likely to remember it as life is happening.

Since we're trying to set the rhythm for a continuous, healthy process, frequently starting a new cycle due to irregularity prevents your system from the continuity of balance.

PERCEPTION

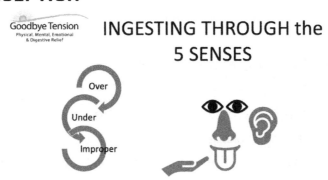

We perceive through our senses. What we perceive is ingested into our Emotional Heart and Mind, and, depending on our past impressions, determines how well we digest what we're ingesting.

What we see, hear, taste, touch, and smell is ingested through the senses, ready to be digested and interpreted. What happens in trauma or adverse experiences is a lack of digestive strength in perception.

Remember the story earlier of going for a walk at dusk with your friend and encountering something on the path. You perceive it's a snake, quickly scream, and jump out of the way. Your friend perceives it as a stick and prepares to brush it out of the way with her foot. Notice the difference in perception. You had some adverse experiences in life and usually had a fear response to things. In contrast, your friend also had adverse experiences in her life but processed these experiences to make them more digestible to her Heart and Mind, which allowed her to have a different response. It's essential to look at yourself and examine your thoughts, actions, and reactions, as they're the key to how you're currently perceiving.

Any overstimulation, understimulation, and improper use of the senses can create an imbalance in perception.

Functions of the mind include:

1. Receiving vibrations: From the sense organs for decision making
2. Controlling: The sense organs from overuse or misuse
3. Self-control: Slowing down the oscillations of different thoughts and focusing on one
4. Chintana: Meditating on various choices and deciding whether to accept a choice or not
5. Vichara: Thinking about the pros and cons of any action
6. Uha: Act of comprehending or inferring
7. Dhyeya: Fit for meditation or to be pondered upon
8. Sankalpa: Setting an intention, developing an action plan to achieve it

Through the Ayurvedic lens, we look at the mind through its qualities in order to use the opposite qualities to bring it into balance.

The three mahagunas (Qualities)

1. Sattva (consciousness): Illuminating, pure, and good, which leads to clarity and mental serenity

2. Rajas (action): Mobility or activity, which makes a person active and energetic, tense, and willful.

3. Tamas (inertia): Dark and restraining, which obstructs and counteracts the tendency of rajas to work and sattva to reveal

The premise for perceptual balance is about understanding which qualities are predominant and which qualities can come in and help create balance.

For example, someone who has more Tamasic qualities will need the quality of Rajas (e.g., dancing) to rise from that heavy state of lethargy.

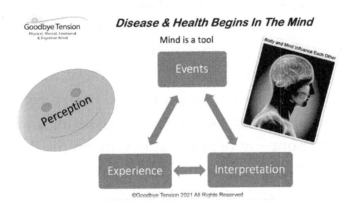

BREATH

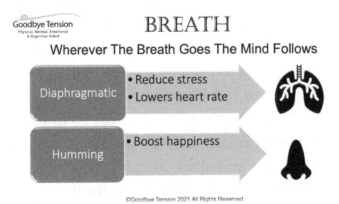

Are you a breath holder? I often wonder how we stay alive when we're in a state of breath-holding. Honestly, we're depriving our entire system of oxygen, and it's happening unconsciously; this is why the need for a breath practice is so relevant.

Wherever the breath goes, the mind follows. If we are holding our breath, where do you think the mind is? It may be frozen, stuck, or heading in a direction we're unaware of. I've found that it's best to check in with the breath to stay aware of the direction the mind is heading. Beginning the day with a deep diaphragmatic breath[1] practice of 5 minutes minimum is a great way to settle the mind and prepare for the day. I make this part of my ritual before I start my day to send fresh oxygenated blood and prana (life force energy) circulating and flowing throughout my being. Trauma interrupts the flow. Beginning the day with a flow of breath is a great way to create stability and safety in your heart, mind, and body. The other breath practice I find helps with mood is the humming or Bhramari Breath.[2] Sit comfortably and allow your eyes to close. Take a breath or two to settle in and notice the state of your mind. When you're ready, inhale and then, for the entire length of your exhalation, make a low- to medium-pitched humming sound in the throat. Notice how the sound waves gently vibrate your tongue, teeth, and sinuses. Imagine the sound is vibrating your entire brain (it really is). Do this practice for six rounds of breath and then, keeping your eyes closed, return to your normal breathing. Notice if anything has changed. I've found that doing this with children is quite helpful. Encouraging children in a fun and playful man-

---

1   https://youtu.be/3SAzl_MmlsE
2   https://youtu.be/XQYWFHPbELM

ner is a great way to learn. For example, "Let's hum to calm down," or "Let's play musical noses."

Check in with your breath upon waking, on your lunch hour, and again before sleep. Aren't you worth 5 minutes morning, noon, and evening? Of course, you are! Commit to making this happen because you're worth it. Once this becomes a habit, you may notice your level of awareness of your breath rise throughout the day, creating even more space for balance and stability. Once you have a stable breath practice, then alternate nostril breathing is a great way to balance your nervous system. Hold your right hand up and curl your index and middle fingers toward your palm. Place your thumb next to your right nostril and your ring finger and pinky by your left. Close the right nostril by pressing gently against it with your thumb, and inhale through the left nostril. The breath should be slow, steady, and full. Now close the left nostril by pressing gently against it with your ring finger and pinky, and open your right nostril by relaxing your thumb and exhale fully with a slow and steady breath. Inhale through the right nostril, close it, and then exhale through the left nostril. That's one complete round. Begin with 5-10 rounds and add more as you feel ready. Remember to keep your breathing slow, easy, and full. There's an imbalance in the nervous system when there has been trauma which may also lead to dis-ease.

FOOD

What to eat? When to eat? How much to eat?

Of these three, which do you think is the most important?

When is the most important.

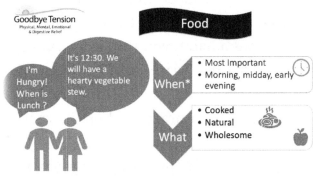

When

There are specific times of day when the elements of nature are at their peak, and if we learn how to align with them, we'll have their support. The element of fire; Pitta represents digestion and transformation. Since digestion is the transformation of nutrients, the ideal time for the largest meal of the day is when Pitta is at its peak; sometime between 12-1:30 pm which is the peak of the Pitta daytime hours of 10 am to 2 pm. The earth and water elements, known as Kapha, are usually when we eat our breakfast and dinner. The Kapha time of day is 6 am to 10 am and 6 pm to 10 pm. That would mean that breakfast would ideally be somewhere around 7-8 am and be a lighter meal than lunch. Dinner ideally would be around 6:30-7:30 pm and be lighter than the lunch meal. Since this element is heavier and represents cohesion, which holds everything together, if we eat more decadent meals during the Kapha hours, we tend to store or retain more. Digestion isn't as strong for transformation during the Kapha hours.

The afternoon snack usually happens during the Vata hours of about 3:30 pm to 4:30 pm, which is about the peak of the 2 pm to 6 pm timeframe.

Since we're connected with nature, there's a natural rhythm. That rhythm shows up in our bodies as well. The heartbeat is a perfect example of this natural rhythm. This rhythm is based on the rhythm of the sun and the moon and the seasons. Notice how the birds naturally wake up and start singing before the sun begins to shine. They're in tune with this rhythm. When you eat is the most important because it relates to the rhythm. The rhythm needs to be set to maintain a healthy and balanced mind-body or come back into balance. When you eat is determined first by when you sleep.

What

The closer from farm to table the better. Our ability to transform is based on how close to nature the food we're ingesting is, which means the least amount of processing, pesticides, chemicals, etc. If you can eat organic, outstanding, or, if not, try to get your food as fresh as possible. If you're living in the United States, the most contaminated food sources are meat and dairy. When considering these options, try to find organic, free-range, grass-fed, humane animal sources.

If you think about it, eating fresh and clean keeps the mind-body that way as well.

Since our digestion is based on fire, known as Agni and transformation, we need to make sure that the food we eat is easy to assimilate in that fire. Ayurveda recommends that we cook our food before eating it, which means trying to minimize raw, uncooked vegetables, grains, and meats.

Imagine that you're cooking raw vegetables or meat on the stove. What level of fire is needed for cooking to happen? Digestion is nothing but cooking. For food to transform, the fire needs to be high enough for cooking to occur. When the fire isn't strong enough, stagnation occurs, and food becomes undigested in the gut, which is the equivalent to the food beginning to spoil on the stove if there isn't enough fire for cooking. We call this undigested material and stagnation Ama, which is a breeding ground for disease. Ama also forms when we sleep late or during the day; overeat; eat late or eat highly processed foods, cold or raw items, and improper food combinations, including fish and milk, equal parts in weight of ghee and honey, as well as, sour fruits with milk. In general, fruit should be eaten by itself. Yes, those yogurt fruit parfaits sold in every coffee shop and convenience store can be a problem.

Try to include more fresh fruits, cooked vegetables, wholesome grains, and easily digestible proteins like mung bean lentils.

How Much

In general, the size of your fist is a portion and it's important to learn to listen to the signal from the body when it feels full. The idea is to only eat to fill half of your stomach, leaving a quarter for liquids and the last quarter for food to move in the stomach for digestion.

The signs of the right quantity of food are:

1. Feeling satisfied
2. Not feeling heavy
3. Should be able to breathe, talk, and walk easily
4. Senses become sharp

How does this relate to our triggers and state of mind?

All our nutrients come from our ability to digest the healthy food we're eating. Those nutrients travel to all our organs, giving energy for them to function. If we're ingesting unwholesome foods or have a low digestive fire, we don't get those nutrients, and, eventually, our body-mind starts to break down. Thus, specific foods can increase the symptoms that show up in the mind.

For example:

- Light
- Cold
- Dry
- Rough
- Raw

foods can increase the element of air and space, known as Vata. Popcorn is a great example to understand the quality of Vata. The elements of air and space elevate when symptoms of anxiousness show up.

- Heavy
- Dense
- Sticky
- Slimy

foods can increase the earth and water elements, known as Kapha, leading to the symptoms of feeling down, heavy, and depressed.

- Spicy
- Sour
- Pungent

foods can increase the elements of fire and water, known as Pitta, leading to symptoms of anger, rage, intensity, etc.

Not everyone will have this experience as there are many key factors, and it's good to know which foods may be a support or a detriment depending on your state of mind and overall current imbalance. When I experience more heaviness, lethargy, and stagnation, where my mind feels dragging, I look at the foods I've eaten to see if adjustments can be made. To have a full Ayurvedic assessment that gives you more of these details specific to your current state and unique mind-body type known as Prakriti and the current imbalance known as your Vikriti, look up Ayurvedic Practitioners or Doctors in your area. You may also reach out to me at Goodbyetension.com.

Foods that can increase the energy of the fight, flight, or freeze response in a system already predisposed to it, known as Rajas, include:

- Alcohol
- Meat
- Sugar
- Highly processed foods
- Garlic, chili peppers, etc.

WATER

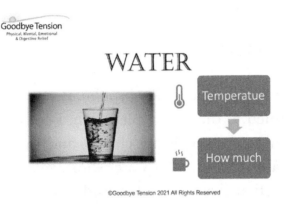

Goodbye Tension
Physical, Mental, Emotional
& Digestive Relief

WATER

Temperatue

How much

©Goodbye Tension 2021 All Rights Reserved

Are you an ice-cold water drinker? A 2-gallon-per-day drinker? This was me at one point in my life. I put out my Agni-digestive fire with the cold temperature and diluted what was left with the amount I was drinking.

We need to kindle our Agni with warm or hot liquids and the amount varies, depending on your Prakriti; unique mind-body type, Vikriti; current imbalance, and activity levels.

What happens when there's not enough water?

Dehydration can occur, causing:

- Dark urine
- Bad breath
- Low brain function
- Lack of concentration
- Dry skin
- Constipation
- Muscle cramps
- Sleepiness
- Headaches
- Dry mouth
- Hunger
- Sugar cravings.

Don't treat your body like you're stranded in the desert, destined to die a horrible death. I see more dehydration these days with my clients, and I often joke with them, asking if there's a water shortage and should I send some their way? All jokes aside, this can create long-term problems in addition to short-term problems. When emotionally and mentally processing, dehydration or hyperhydration is one more stressor on an already stressed-out system. Too much or too little is both a problem and can create a breeding ground for dis-ease.

When

If we drink a lot of water before our meal this can also dilute the digestive fire so try sipping your water throughout the day avoiding right before and during the meal.

Beginning your morning with a warm cup of water will not only facilitate a bowel movement but also prepare the rhythm for water intake throughout the day.

Try the Daily Self-Care Tracker Worksheet below to see what your current rhythm is and work toward making adjustments when necessary.

Goodbye Tension
Physical, Mental, Emotional
& Digestive Relief

Daily Self-Care Tracker

Date:

Upon waking, I feel...

Breathing Practice	Movement/Exercise	Breakfast When: What:	Water Intake

Midday, I feel....

Breathing Practice	Work/Study	Lunch When: What:	Water Intake

Evening, I feel...

Breathing Practice	Chores	Dinner When: What:	Water Intake

How would you have preferred the day been?

What can you change within for a better experience?

Did you resolve negative emotions, experiences or perceptions using the pocket guide?

Preparing for sleep, I feel....

Breathing Practice	**Self-Care**
Type:	Type:
How long:	Went to sleep at:

The five key ingredients for stability and balance in mind and body are Lifestyle/Routine, Perception, Breath, Food and Water.

 Build a strong foundation so you can process the deeper mental and emotional impressions for a healthier relationship with yourself and others.

Chapter 15

Hope for you!

My hope for you is that you'll create the most beautiful, loving relationship with yourself. The benefits of this include healthier relationships coming into your life and healing the relationships at home. The family unit then goes out into the community from a healthier place and creates even healthier communities until community after community heals and circles the globe.

Where I am today

The role of a grandmother is extraordinary. As a 43-year-old grandmother to three, I enjoy sparking creativity and imagination along with valuable life wisdom through storytelling with gnomes and fairytale creatures and using the elements of nature carrying on my grandmother's tradition.

I take my healing very seriously for the sake of their future. The more work I do on myself, the more awareness we have as a family, and, gratefully, my family is in alignment with healing their wounds. Together, we're unstoppable when we have courage, commitment, and humility to show those things we try to avoid. When our hearts open, we begin a flow that cleanses and creates space for something new to blossom. I continually notice a change in my daughters after I've healed something in myself. Often, I'll share what I healed not only to inspire but also to show my imperfection so that we break the cycle of perfectionism. Sometimes, the healing that's done may instantly heal something in the next bloodline generation. Because of this, I keep at it even when it gets challenging. I don't want my daughters, grandkids, or great-grandkids to have to work so hard at healing. If I can do it and make their lives easier by reducing the possibilities of dysfunction, then that's a great legacy to leave behind.

My Goodbye Tension practice continues to evolve as I evolve. My ability to learn and my passion for health has led me down the path of becoming a Doctor of Ayurveda, specializing in the mind, known as Sattvavajaya Chikitsa (Ayurvedic Psychotherapy) and Yuktivyapashraya Chikitsa (Ayurvedic Rational Therapy).

My husband and I have been together for more than a decade, aligned in our commitment to healing ourselves and creating a conscious family environment.

Both daughters have found healthier partners than I had the first time around and are now raising their own families with the same healing intent.

My future aspirations are continuing motivational speaking, TED talks, and any opportunities where large groups of people need to hear the healing message and ignite inspiration for change.

When I look back at what I was born into, lived through, and where I am today, I feel such sincere gratitude for all the guiding lights along the way. This story could have turned out very different had I given up on myself.

You are in the driver's seat of your life. Do you like where you are headed or the direction you are going? If not, then turn around, look within and create a new path for your life.

May you never give up on yourself because this journey of life begins with you!

 Never give up.

 Believe you can do this.

 A new experience of life is possible.

 Remember your courage, commitment to yourself, and be ready for change.

Goodbye Tension
Physical, Mental, Emotional
& Digestive Relief

I'm TRIGGERED! Pocket Guide

Step 1: Stop.

Don't make decisions!

Excuse yourself or ask for a time out (self-responsibility is very empowering)

BREATHE with two short inhales and one long exhale.

Step 2: Locate

Locate three objects, preferably that are related to nature or that represent the current time and space.

Keeping the eyes moving creates a presence that can reduce the reactive fight, flight, or freeze response.

BREATHE with two short inhales and one long exhale.

Step 3: Identify

Identify your well-wishers-helpful people.

Giving the mind the remembrance of allies is positive, which may counteract the negative experience.

BREATHE with 1 long, slow, deep inhale, and a slow exhale.

EDHIR (R)

Step 4: Explore

What's the primary feeling you're having?
(Write it down, so you don't get distracted by your mind maze)

If you use your smartphone, this will create a timestamp for the note, which is excellent for tracking patterns.

BREATHE with one long, slow, deep inhale, and one slow exhale.

Step 5: Discover

Identify your trigger down to the simplest form.

Was it a smell, sound, taste, thought, word, touch, something you saw, or body language? (Write it down)

BREATHE with two quick inhales and one slow exhale.

Step 6: Get Big

Get big, real big. Imagine you're so big that you have a 360-degree view of the part of you that's triggered.

You're now the Guardian of that triggered aspect. At first, it's helpful to imagine a big you and a small you.

BREATHE with long, slow inhales and exhales.

Step7: Heal

As you witness the triggered, small version of yourself feeling _____triggered by _____, What wisdom and healing does this version of you need?

How can you offer safety and security so that the higher wisdom from the Guardian or big you will be heard by the small you?

You're essentially building trust with this aspect of your-self and taking full guardianship, which includes show-ing them a bigger picture, a different perspective with the love and protection they need to feel safe.

Remember to make them a promise that you're taking full responsibility and won't abandon them. If you miss this step, it may be difficult for integration to begin.

BREATHE with long, slow inhales and exhales.

Step 8: Integrate

Healing has happened, and it's time to integrate the disconnected, healed aspect with the present and evolved version of yourself.

Hold hands with this part of you and look deeply into each other's eyes until the two of you become one.

BREATHE deeply as you observe and feel this union happening.

Step 9: Test

Imagine you're back in the place where you began, triggered by_____ and feeling_____.

Do you get triggered by this?
If yes, repeat steps 1-8. If not, move to step 10.

Step 10: Relate

This is where you get to know the upgraded version of yourself.

You tested your work and upgraded from being triggered to being empowered.

You may relate differently, be open to possibilities, and try not to put limitations on yourself.

Take yourself on a date to get to know the new you. Congratulations, you did it. CELEBRATE!!!!!

Free Gift

Download your free Abundance Beyond Trauma
Workbook here.

https://www.goodbyetension.com/abundance-beyond-trauma

About the Artists

Susanne Kurwig is an artist/painter from Germany.

She paints floral impressions inspired by nature, her garden, the sky, earth, sun, and wind. When she paints, she follows the stream of creativity, stimulated by flora; she abstracts these natural impressions into color-intensive, dynamic surfaces and combines those with filigree forms and structures. The colors and the light, the energy, and the dynamics of the expression are vital to her. Susanne loves color contrasts and a robust rhythm which she combines into a fantastic harmony with each painting.

Susanne also likes to paint faces and figures from time to time. She combined her floral abstract painting style with a figure to represent Jeannine's story for this painting. A journey from darkness into light.

For more information, please visit her website, www.susannekurwig.com.

Amanda Kritzberg is the owner of Daylong Daydreams, a creative business that she uses to showcase her original artwork and projects. Her artwork emphasizes the color, beauty, and enchantment of everyday life. You'll find paintings with whimsical forest creatures, rainbow-inspired abstracts, and cotton candy skies. Exaggerated hues and washes of color are used as the focal point to create works that are simple in form yet complex in color and detail. She believes that by looking at life through a creative, optimistic lens, ordinary sights can become whimsical scenes, and everyday objects can inspire the imagination.

This artwork was inspired by and created specifically for Jeannine's book. For more information on the artist, please visit her website at www.daylongdaydreams.com.

Art By Amanda Kritzberg

Art By Susanne Kurwig

About the Author

 Jeannine Rashidi is a highly qualified health and wellness practitioner. She opened her Goodbye Tension practice in 2003, focused on alleviating the core of physical, digestive, emotional, and mental tension. Her commitment to empower and inspire her clients toward awakening the healer within has been a passion for the last 18 years. She also brings her personal experiences of healing trauma, including the EDHIR® process she created to guide her clients toward integrating the Heart and Mind after the disconnect from trauma and adverse life experiences.

Jeannine is also an Ayurvedic Practitioner finishing her last year in the Ayurvedic Doctorate program at Kerala Ayurveda Academy. She has apprenticed under Dr. Jayarajan Kodikannath since 2016, traveled to Kerala to directly experience the roots of Ayurveda, and is an ongoing Samskritam (Sanskrit) student to enable her to study the source Ayurvedic books directly.

Jeannine is a devoted wife, mother, and recent grandmother. In her spare time, she enjoys cooking, photography, meditation, time dedicated to family, spiritual practice, and creating stories with gnomes, and other fairytale creatures, continuing the tradition from her late grandmother Laurel.

Interested in working together on your healing journey?

Online appointments are offered worldwide.

Inquire at Goodbyetension.com
or email byetension@gmail.com

Can You Help?

Thank You for Reading My Book!

I appreciate all of your feedback and love hearing what you have to say.

I need your input to make the next version of this book and my future books better. Please leave me an honest review on Amazon, letting me know what you thought of the book.

Thanks so much!

Jeannine L. Rashidi